THE EARLY HISTORY OF EGYPT,

FROM

THE OLD TESTAMENT,

HERODOTUS, MANETHO,

AND

THE HIEROGLYPHICAL INSCRIPTIONS.

By SAMUEL SHARPE.

Τοισι μεν νυν ὑπ' Αἰγυπτιων λεγομενοισι χρασθω ὅτεῳ τα τοιαυτα πιθανα ἐστι· ἐμοι δε παρα παντα τον λογον ὑποκειται, ὅτι τα λεγομενα ὑπ' ἑκαστων ἀκοῃ γραφω. Herod. *Euterpe*, 123.

ISBN: 978-1-63923-670-1

All Rights reserved. No part of this book maybe reproduced without written permission from the publishers, except by a reviewer who may quote brief passages in a review to be printed in a newspaper or magazine.

Printed: February 2023

Published and Distributed By:
Lushena Books
607 Country Club Drive, Unit E
Bensenville, IL 60106
www.lushenabks.com

ISBN: 978-1-63923-670-1

PREFACE.

THE object of the Author in the following pages has been to collect out of the writings of the ancients every particular relating to the History of Egypt, before the conquest of that country by the Persians. The collection is no doubt far from complete, but probably contains all the most important passages now extant; and, however unsatisfactory these fragments may be thought, upon these, assisted by the remaining monuments of the country, the History of Egypt at that early period must rest.

The extracts from each historian are placed separately, so that, in the words of Herodotus quoted in the title page, " each person may use those which he thinks may be relied upon;" and the remarks which are added, with a view to explain the extracts, and to show how far the account of one historian is consistent with that of another, are also kept distinct, so that the value of the quotations may not be lessened by the errors of the criticisms.

The information derived from the hieroglyphical inscriptions, which have been unlocked to us by the ingenuity of Dr. Young, forms a very valuable addition and confirmation to the accounts of the Greek historians, and one which we may with confidence expect to see increased, now that the attention of travellers has been directed to it; and the

Author hopes that the present attempt may serve to point out to them what the doubtful points in Egyptian history are, which might possibly be illustrated by the discovery of other inscriptions.

The enumeration of the principal buildings erected in each reign is arranged chronologically, and is nearly the only evidence of the comparative wealth and power of the kings; in this list is included their statues in the British Museum, which to us are a more important testimony than many larger works, which we only know through the descriptions of travellers.

The conclusions arrived at will be found occasionally to differ from those of Champollion, Wilkinson, Heeren, and other eminent antiquarians who have written upon the same subject,—and always from the same cause, that the author has followed the Greek historians more closely than has been usually done.

A few particulars, with the dates and order of succession of the Ptolemies, have been added, though without any attempt at making a complete history of that interesting dynasty, for which the materials are more abundant than they are for the earlier races of kings, and whose series of coins reminds us of that desideratum in the early history of Egypt: no coin of the country is known before the time of Alexander the Great, nor have the Greek authors even given us any information respecting the payments, or measures of value.

A slight account of the Mythology naturally follows, because the same researches, both in the ancient authors and in the hieroglyphics, are required for the mythological as for the historical enquiry.

Some notice of the Hieroglyphics, of the Enchorial writing, of the Coptic and Ethiopic languages, seemed to be required by the subject; not only because part of the historical information is obtained by means of the first of these, but because the languages throw considerable light on the various races of inhabitants of Egypt and its borders.

But the part which the author feels has most need of explanation, to save him from the charge of presumption, is the essays on the dates of the Trojan War and Jewish Exodus. There are two epochs in the history of the Jews, and two in the history of Greece, upon which the chronology of Egypt principally rests: these are the times of Moses, Solomon, Cambyses, and the Trojan War. The accession of Cambyses is as well known, by means of the eclipses of the moon observed at Babylon, as is the accession of George III.; the time of Solomon's reign is nearly as well known; but considerable doubt hangs over the other epochs, which the Author is not so presumptuous as to suppose that he has in any degree dispelled; but he thought it desireable to state the grounds upon which he had assigned dates to those events. The time of the Trojan War is perhaps the least uncertain of the two, but then it is the least important, because the enquiry in strictness ought to be, not when that war took place, but when did Manetho, who dates from it as an epoch, suppose that it took place. But however antiquarians may differ about a few minor points, the agreement between the various authorities will be seen to be in the highest degree satisfactory. The fragments of Manetho, which are quoted by Josephus as a valuable testimony to the truth of the Jewish history, are confirmed by the list of kings contained in the Tablet of Abydus in particular, and by every historical inscription which can be compared with them: Herodotus and the later books of the Old Testament strongly illustrate one another, and further light is thrown upon both of them by several passages in later historians: and though we have no contemporary authority early enough to be compared with the account of Egypt in the Old Testament before the Jewish Exodus, yet the splendid buildings which were erected in the centuries immediately following satisfactorily confirm the account of the high state of civilization observed there by Abraham and Joseph.

The modern authors whose works have been principally made use of, and require a particular acknowledgement, are Dr. Young, M. Champollion, and Mr. Wilkinson.

The Author has to apologize for the omission, in page 41, of the following lines of the fragments of Manetho:

19th Dynasty,—Of Diospolis.

1. Sethos, 51 or 55 years, called also Rameses from his father or grandfather.

2. Rapsaces, or Ramesses, 61 or 66 years; he maintained an army of cavalry, and a fleet.

3. Ammenephthes, or Amenophes, 8 or 20 years.

4. Rameses, 60 years.

5. Ammenemes, 5 years.

6. Thuoris, who is called by Homer Polybus, the husband of Alcandra; in whose time Troy was taken; reigned 7 years.

Together, 209 years.

So far the second book of Manetho, containing 96 kings and 2121 years.

Canonbury, 8th March, 1836.

CONTENTS.

	Page
Introduction	1
Notices relating to the early history of Egypt, drawn from	
The Old Testament	8
Herodotus	17
His chronology	26
Diodorus Siculus	27
Compared with Herodotus	33
Manetho	34
The Tablet of Kings at Abydus	54
Compared with Manetho	56
The Egyptian Buildings	61
The Pyramids	78
Eratosthenes	81
Flavius Josephus	84
Aristotle	85
Dicæarchus	86
Strabo	86
Tacitus	91
Pausanias	92
Pliny	94
Valerius Flaccus	100
Homer	101
Hesiod	102
Plutarch	102
Ammianus Marcellinus	103

CONTENTS.

	Page
Xenophon	104
Quintus Curtius	104
Porphyry	105
On the Egyptian Year	111
The Zodiac of Dendera	113
Hipparchus and Ptolemy	115
Censorinus	116
Theon	118
On the Physical Character of the Egyptians	121
On the Mythology of the Egyptians	124
On the Coptic Language	133
On the Ethiopic Language	138
On the Hieroglyphics and Hieratic Writing	141
Clemens Alexandrinus	147
Horus Apollo	150
On the Enchorial Language	152
On the Date of the Trojan War	158
On the Date of the Jewish Exodus	163
Chronological Table	167
Description of the Plates	169

ERRATUM.—Page 71, line 4, *for* which he, *read* which can be.

THE
EARLY HISTORY OF EGYPT.

INTRODUCTION.

OF the early history of Egypt the accounts which have come down to us are so bald, and so far from meeting with universal belief, that it seems to be the best course to lay the whole before the enquirer in the separate forms in which the fragments exist, rather than attempt to frame one connected account, which can never be satisfactory unless reliance be placed on most of the original authors. In the case of Egypt there is an additional reason for this course; the original authors are but few, and their accounts are so different that they must, if all true, relate either to different countries, or parts of the country, or to different times.

The principal sources of information are, first, the Old Testament, which of course, from the geographical position of the countries, when it contains information about Egypt, must be understood to mean Lower Egypt, at least whenever the two parts of Egypt were under different kings.

Secondly, Herodotus, who tells us that he obtained his information from the priests at Memphis and the Greek colonists in the Delta; hence his history also is that of Lower Egypt.

Herodotus and the Old Testament agree entirely in their chronology. Herodotus has not given us any regular history or series of kings' names before the reign of Solomon, and after this time the first king mentioned by name is the same in each, *viz.* Sesostris, or Shishak; and probably for this reason, that he was the first great king that reigned in Lower Egypt.

Thirdly, Diodorus Siculus, who lived four hundred years later than Herodotus: he does not say where he got his information; but he agrees sufficiently with the history of Herodotus to prove that he had only heard of those kings who ruled at Memphis.

Fourthly, Manetho, whose list of kings runs back to a very early period: of a considerable part of this we can make no use, having nothing to compare it with; but, if we begin with the expulsion of the Hycsos and the rise of the great Theban empire, he leads us through a list of kings whose greatness and wealth is proved by the monuments which remain to us. On the decline of Upper Egypt, about the time of Solomon, he furnishes us with the names and length of reigns of the Pharaohs of Lower Egypt, and in no particular does he differ with the Old Testament or with Herodotus; though, indeed, in the principal points he does not admit of any comparison with them, that is, in his kings of Upper Egypt.

Fifthly, The genealogical tablet of kings, discovered by Mr. W. J. Bankes at Abydos, contains a list of the kings of Upper Egypt, probably, when perfect, sixty-four in number. Of the first portion of these we can make no use, from not being able to read their names; but the last portion, containing the names of the Theban kings from the rise of that monarchy till nearly the last who bore the name of Rameses, and its fall under the Ethiopian invasion, agrees even more exactly than could be expected with the names of Manetho's kings, and quite confirms his statement, that he got his information from the monuments of the country. The tablet contains no kings of Lower Egypt, and therefore cannot be compared with the Old Testament or Herodotus. Nothing is known respecting its age, but we may conclude that it was made in the reign of the last king mentioned in it, probably about 800 B.C.

Sixthly, The remaining buildings of Egypt are generally covered with hieroglyphical inscriptions, which are in all cases sufficiently understood for us to know by what king these wonderful works of art were built; and, by comparing these names with the tablet of Abydos, and again with Manetho's history, we obtain the wished-for knowledge, for which indeed chronology and the mechanical part of history is principally valuable, namely the order of succession, and the approximate time at which the stupendous monuments of Upper Egypt were erected.

The following is a list of the principal authors who have either written expressly on the subject or have left notices respecting the early history of Egypt, which are made use of in the following pages.

B.C.	1400 or 1200	The Books of Genesis and Exodus.
	820	Homer and Hesiod.
	800	The tablet of kings at Abydos.
	580	Jeremiah, Books of Kings and Chronicles.
	430	Herodotus, visited Egypt.
	260	Manetho, an Egyptian.
	200	Eratosthenes.
	40	Diodorus Siculus, visited Egypt.
	40	Strabo, visited Egypt.
A.C.	40	Quintus Curtius, visited Egypt.
	60	Pliny.
	90	Tacitus.
	100	Plutarch, visited Egypt.
	160	Pausanias.

From these authors I have, I believe, extracted all the passages which relate directly to the chronology of Egypt or contain the names of Egyptian kings before the Persian invasion.

We learn from the Old Testament that, while the Jews, the earliest nation that has handed down to us the history of its rise and civilization, were yet a tribe of wandering shepherds, under Abraham, depending solely upon the unbought gifts of nature, who, when they had exhausted one district, instead of cultivating it, drove off their flocks in search of another, the Egyptians were acquainted with agriculture, and all those arts of civilization and government, and notions of property, which usually belong to nations which have been long settled and civilized. This we find confirmed in a striking manner by the architectural remains that have survived the ravages of above thirty centuries; for, while the Jews, under the immediate successors of Joshua, were still warring with the Canaanites for the possession of the country, or perhaps even while they were yet slaves in Egypt, Egypt itself possessed palaces, temples, porticoes, obelisks, statues, and canals, which are even now the admiration of the world. And though the Jews never allowed that they learned their arts of civilization from their cruel task-masters, but owed them a grudge which lasted till the growing power of Assyria made it prudent for them to forget it, yet the Greeks have abundantly borne testimony to how much the world is indebted to the Egyptians for architecture, geometry, agriculture, irrigation, letters, and paper (*qua constat hominum immortalitas*, says Pliny). Indeed the earliest *express assertion* of the *immortality of the soul* is found in the statement by Herodotus of the opinions held by the Egyptians (lib. ii. 123).

That most remarkable custom of embalming the dead, to which the numerous mummies yet bear witness, they practised even in the earliest ages; it is mentioned in Genesis, chap. 1., by Herodotus, and by all succeeding writers.

But the buildings are the principal evidence of the extent to which they had cultivated the arts of civilization and production. From their vast size and number we are immediately led to consider the populousness of the country, the number of hands, and the mechanical knowledge employed in raising these monuments, and the complete cultivation of the soil required to feed such a population; and this again is corroborated by the extent of the canals, lakes, and other works used for irrigation.

The quantity of mathematical knowledge required to make the waters of the Nile useful for this purpose over such an extent of country, from the highest nilometer at Elephantine to that great reservoir the lake of Mœris, and again over the alluvial plain of the Delta, can best be judged of by considering the number of published works on hydrostatics, and on the force of running water, that have been brought into existence by the rise in the bed of the Po, and by the dykes of Holland; and by recollecting that the draining of the Pontine marshes has baffled the attempts of the Roman engineers from the time of the emperors to the present day.

Indeed, Egypt teems with evidence of the great civilization of its early inhabitants, and with materials to awaken our curiosity and spur our enquiries into its letters and history; and our disappointment is of course fully equal to our curiosity when we find, from every fresh advance which is made in the reading of hieroglyphics, how little the priests thought worth the recording, in that laborious and durable manner which has already survived thirty centuries, beyond the titles of their gods and the particulars of the sacred offerings to their shrines.

In the following pages the events are all made more modern than in the system of chronology usually adopted, and yet we go back to the year B.C. 1600, before we come to one of those heroes whose exaggerated actions prove that we are beyond the bounds of exact history,—Osirtesen I., the Sesostris or Sesonkosis of Manetho (not of Herodotus), the Sesoosis of Diodorus Siculus, who conquered India beyond the Ganges.

Women were allowed to succeed to the throne at a very early time, a circumstance that proves a quiet succession in the sovereignty and polished manners in the people. Indeed, in giving to the female name the precedence on all occasions, as in the case even of Isis and Osiris, they exceeded the politeness of moderns.

Of the form of Government we know but little, and that little relates to Lower Egypt; though it is probable that the two regions did not differ in this respect: it was monarchical, but very far from despotic in the bad meaning of the word; for a king surrounded by an hereditary order of soldiers and an hereditary order of priests, and these possessed of civil power, must have felt himself a good deal checked by his aristocracy. And, without supposing the assembly of elected judges to have possessed the important privileges of legislation and control of the monarch which we now annex to the idea of a representative chamber, it can hardly have been of less importance in those respects than the old French parliaments, which were not elected. But the few facts which we possess, respecting the limitation of the royal power, are strengthened by their adoption of the English constitutional axiom, and exactly in the sense in which we now use it, that the king could do no wrong: his advisers bore the blame. He was himself, in some cases, of the priestly order, as we learn from Herodotus and the hieroglyphical inscriptions. The two privileged orders held their estates free of rent or taxes, while the rest of the people paid a fifth of the produce to the crown. Each city had a tutelary divinity, after whom it was often named; and in some cases, most probably in all, the chief priest, in the temple of this god, was the chief magistrate of the city. As the priests were the hereditary and sole depositaries of all learning, we must also suppose that they filled the judicial and magisterial offices, as well as the learned professions.

The enquiry into the political condition of any people who have left behind them works worthy of admiration, is of the highest moral importance. The pyramids of Lower Egypt, requiring for their erection the least quantity of architectural knowledge, no elegance of design, no taste in the detail, might possibly have been the work of men driven by task-masters to their daily labour; but that the palaces, tombs, and temples of Upper Egypt, which present to us the earliest known instances of architecture, sculpture, and painting; the colossal statues of Amenothph and Rameses, requiring considerable anatomical knowledge for the original design, and a mechanical skill in transferring that design from the model to the block of stone exceeding perhaps even that of the Greeks themselves; the vast works for irrigation; and the correct division of the calendar, requiring great knowledge of mathematics, and this at a time when no other nation, certainly none with whom they were connected, was in an equally cultivated state;—that these should have been the works of a people suffering under political disadvantages would contradict all our observations on the human mind and its powers.

A tree is known by its fruit; and every circumstance, of which Herodotus and Diodorus have related many, that leads us to believe that the kingdom of Thebes, at the time that it was one of those favored spots in which the human mind has been most expanded, enjoyed also the blessings of good government, must be gratifying to the historical enquirer.

THE OLD TESTAMENT.

In the Book of Genesis, ch. x. v. 6, &c. we have the following account of the descent of the Egyptians, and of all the nations with whom they were most closely connected in war and peace.

" And the sons of HAM,
 Cush, [Arabia and Assyria.
 and Mizraim, [Egypt.
 and Phut,
 and Canaan; [The aborigines of the land of Canaan.
" And the sons of Cush,
  Seba, [Petra. See Isaiah, xlv. 14.
  and Havilah, [Armenia?
  and Sabtah,
  and Raamah,
  and Sabtechah,
  and Nimrod (the Hunter, and the beginning of his kingdom was Babel), [the Assyrian empire.
" The sons of Raamah,
  Sheba, [The incense country of Arabia, whose queen
   visited Solomon.
  and Dedan.
" And Mizraim begat
  Ludim, [Ethiopians, before the Cushite invasion?
  and Anamim,
  and Lehabim, [Africa to the west of the Nile, Lybia.

and Naphtuhim, [Arabia Nabatæa, of which Petra was the capital.

and Pathrusim, [Upper Egypt. See Is. xi. 11; Jer. xliv. 1.

and Casluhim, [On the coast between Egypt and the Philistines.

" (Out of whom came Philistim), [The Philistines, the inhabitants of the southern part of Canaan.

and Caphtorim, [The Copts, Coptos.

" These are the sons of Ham, after their families, after their tongues, in their countries, in their nations." &c.

The explanation of this history of the descent of the nations that were descendants of Ham is attended with very great difficulty; and this difficulty is further increased by our finding that, at the earliest period to which our knowledge reaches, in most of the countries here described as peopled by descendants of Cush, an Arabic dialect was spoken, which, from its close analogy to Hebrew, would have led us to call them sons of Shem. It might be conjectured that the aborigines were Cushites, and that after the time of Abraham the countries were peopled by Arabs; but this would not alter the case, because there is reason to believe that the people called Cushites in the later books of the Old Testament spoke Arabic; hence we must conclude that Arabic was the language of the sons of Cush, and that Coptic was confined to the sons of Mizraim.

Of the four great divisions, three may be considered as known; and, as Phut is not subdivided into tribes, we may suppose it some nation more distant and less connected with the Jews. With the subdivisions of the Land of Canaan we are not here cóncerned; they were the tribes which the Jews found in possession of the promised land. Cush and Mizraim are the object of the present enquiry, and only a part of their subdivisions are understood.

In the want of knowledge where to place some of the nations of the Cushites, we are not justified in placing any of them to the west of the Red Sea, but must rather suppose that the migration of Cushites across its southern end into Ethiopia took place at a later period.

Ludim is, throughout the Old Testament, translated by the Septuagint Lydians; and in Jeremiah, xlvi. we have the additional phrase, Lydians " that bend the bow." Bochard considers that they inhabited Ethiopia. In Isaiah, lxvi. 19, they are mentioned in connection with Egypt and Pul (the kingdom of Phylæ or Elephantine). According to Strabo, as hereafter quoted, the Ethiopians fought with a bow of four cubits length. The Philistines, we see, were not aborigines in the country to which they afterwards gave their name, but entered Palestine from Arabia, probably later than the Jews did, being of Egyptian origin.

Genesis, xii.—Abraham journeyed into Egypt, when the famine made it difficult for him to feed his flocks in his own country: thus the first mention of Egypt is on account of its fertility. The Pharaoh on the throne at that early time was surrounded with princes and servants.

Genesis, xxi. 9, &c.—God said unto Abraham, " and also of the son of the bond-woman [Ishmael, the son of Hagar the Egyptian] will I make a great nation, because he is thy seed." "And he dwelt in the wilderness and became an archer: and he dwelt in the wilderness of Paran, and his mother took him a wife out of the land of Egypt."

Here is distinct notice of the existence of a great nation, of a mixt race between the Egyptians and the Chaldeans, that dwelt on the western side of Arabia, which we shall meet with again at the time of the Exodus. It was from this circumstance probably that the Arabs had their name ערב, mixt people (see forward), without which I should have supposed they had been so named in contempt, as the word also means *rabble*.

Genesis, xxxix. to Exodus, xv.—The next time Egypt is mentioned is in the next famine, when the Hebrews, the great grandchildren of Abraham, again went there, to buy corn. They found that the Pharaoh had set Joseph, a slave of their own nation, over the land; his Egyptian name was Zaphnath Paaneah; he had married the daughter of Potipherah, the priest of On. The name of the Pharaoh is not mentioned. Joseph's office was to gather up the corn in years of plenty against the coming famine which he had foretold. The Hebrews were well treated, in compliment to their countryman Joseph; and though, like all other shepherds, a despised race, with whom the Egyptians would not eat, they were allowed to dwell in the land of Goshen, which was in the district of Rameses. The famine was so severe, and lasted so long, that the Egyptians not only gave their money and cattle for corn, but surrendered their land to the king, which from that time they only held as tenants of the crown, paying one-fifth of the produce as a rent; the priests, however, retained their lands.

When that generation had passed away, " there arose up a new king," probably of a new dynasty, " over Egypt, who knew not Joseph," and had no recollection of his services. He was jealous of the increase of the Hebrews: he persecuted them by setting severe task-masters over them, and requiring heavy tasks from them in husbandry, brickmaking, and building the strong cities Pithom and Rameses; and because this did not lessen the numbers of this despised and subject race, he began to put to death the male infants. Upon this, miraculous plagues were sent upon the Egyptians; and lastly, when the first-born in every family had died in one night, the Hebrews were allowed to depart home from Egypt. They journeyed from Rameses to Succoth, thence to Pi-Hahiroth between Migdol and the Red Sea, and thence entered Arabia. This was in the third generation after they settled in Egypt under Joseph, and the sixth generation after Abraham visited the country.

We find that at this time Egypt was a well-peopled and well-cultivated country, with numerous cities, under a despotic monarch, surrounded by officers of his court and a life-guard, of which the captain was named Potiphar. There was a ceremonial at audience, a distinction of ranks, a state prison, and a prime minister. Great buildings were carried on, at which their slaves worked under task-masters. There was an order of priests, set apart from the rest of the people, who probably filled the civil offices of government: the priest of Midian and the priest of On no doubt ruled over the cities of those names. The wise men, sorcerers, and magicians were that class of priests who kept the sacred and secret knowledge. There were physicians or embalmers of the dead. The royal army contained chosen captains and horsemen and chariots. Their attention to agriculture, and consequent fixt notions of property, made them hold the shepherd or nomad tribes in abhorrence, as marauders, only less piratical than the hunting tribes. This deeprooted hostility, which has always existed between the nations of agriculturists and the nations of herdsmen, is to be traced in the history of Cain and Abel. We may remark that the herdsmen had, on the other hand, as fixt a dislike towards the hunting tribes, the descendants of Nimrod, who afterwards formed the great Assyrian empire, as the Egyptian cultivators of the soil had of the herdsmen.

Pith-om was no doubt the same place as On, being preceded by the Coptic article; and if we had not the authority of the Septuagint for On being Heliopolis, I should conjecture that Ra-meses were Helio-polis, Ra being the Coptic, as Helios the Greek, for Sun, and that Pith-om were Memphis, HM or Hom being the hieroglyphical name for Memphis in the Rosetta stone.

Exodus, xii. 37, 38.—The Jews went out of Egypt in number "600,000 men beside children: and a mixed multitude (ערב) went up also with them."

This mixed multitude were of course some of the inhabitants of Lower Egypt, who were expelled on the occasion of the change of dynasty which caused the expulsion of the Jews. As we cannot believe that they were incorporated into the Jewish nation, and marched with them into Palestine, we should, in the absence of further information, be led to conjecture that they must have settled in Arabia Nabatæa; but we fortunately have sufficient proof that this mixt race of colonists did settle in Arabia Nabatæa, the first country they entered. They are spoken of in the following passages as Arabs, as a nation in the desert bordering upon Egypt.

Ezekiel, xxx. 4, 5.—" And the sword shall come upon Egypt, and great pain shall be in Ethiopia, when the slain shall fall in Egypt, and they shall take away her multitude, and her foundations shall be broken down. Ethiopia, and Libya, and Lydia, and all the mingled people (ערב), and Chub, and the men of the land that is in league, shall fall with them by the sword."

Jeremiah, xxv. 19, &c.—" Pharaoh king of Egypt, and his servants and his princes and all his people; and all the mingled people (ערב), and all the kings of the land of Uz; and all the kings of the land of the Philistines, and Ashkelon, and Azzah, and Ekron, and the remnant of Ashdod; Edom, and Moab, and the children of

Ammon; and all the kings of Tyrus, and all the kings of Zidon, and the kings of the isles which are beyond the sea; Dedan, and Tema, and Buz, and all in the utmost corners, and all the kings of Arabia, and all the kings of the mingled people (ערב) that dwell in the desert."

Perhaps it was from the nature of the place in which the mingled people settled, that a desert was called ערב; and though this particular country was in the Old Testament more strictly called Horeb, חרב (Deut. iv.), a word considered radically different, yet in the Chaldee dialect ערב is the name of Arabia itself: ערבי Arabs: and so in the Syriac version of the New Testament, Acts, ii. 11., ערביא, Arabia; and Matthew, xxiv. 27, מערבא, the west; proving that only the western corner of what we call Arabia was meant, as the rest was not to the west of the land where Syriac was spoken.

I am not aware on what ground Horeb, the country in which Mount Sinai stood, came to be itself considered as a mountain by some of our writers and map-makers.

1 Kings, ix.—Solomon marries the daughter of a Pharaoh, who besieges and burns the city of Gezer (Gazar), and gives it as a dower with his daughter: consequently, this king must have been master of Lower Egypt. Solomon buys chariots, horses, and fine linen from Egypt; the price of a chariot is 600 shekels of silver, and of a horse 150. Tahpenes was the name of the wife of the Pharaoh, who probably was Shishak; as when Jeroboam fled from Solomon, Shishak was on the throne of Egypt.

2 Chronicles, xii.—In the fifth year of Rehoboam (B.C. 970) Shishak marched against Jerusalem with 1,200 chariots, 60,000 horsemen, and foot-soldiers without number, of Lubims, Sukkiims, and Cushites: he took Jerusalem, and the other fortified cities, and took away the treasures from the Temple.

Twenty-five years later, in the tenth year of king Asa, Zerah the Cushite attacked Judea with an army of a thousand thousands of men (*i.e.* very many thousands) and 300 chariots. Asa defeated them in the valley of Zephathah at Mareshah (lat. 31° 40'), utterly routed them, pursued them to Gerar (lat. 31° 30'), and carried back much plunder from that neighbourhood. This, however, leaves us uncertain on which side of the Red Sea these Cushites dwelt; the number of his army proves the extent of country over which Zerah ruled, and Jahn in his Hebrew Commonwealth conjectures, but without any authority, that he was king of Cush on each side of the Red Sea: but even if this were the case, his march must have been on the Arabian side, as we shall hereafter see that it was improbable that he could have marched through Egypt, or ruled over Egypt. We see that his territory extended over a large part of southern Palestine, as the victorious king of Judæa treated those provinces as the enemy's country. (2 Chronicles, xiv.)

2 Kings, xvii.—In the twelfth year of king Ahaz (B.C. 729) we find that Hoshea king of Israel left off paying tribute to the king of Assyria, as he had been accustomed, and courted the alliance of So or Seve (סוא) king of Egypt, who must have been a very powerful king, to have been thought able to assist the Jews in withstanding their warlike and increasing neighbour the king of Assyria. This was done against the advice of Isaiah (chap. xxxi.), who strongly recommended them to trust to God and their own efforts, instead of endeavouring to exist by trimming between Egypt and Assyria. He foresaw (chap. xix. 23) that the growing strength of these great kingdoms would bring them into collision, and wished the Jews not to take part with either, at any rate not with the weaker and more distant; and he looked forward, though, alas, too sanguinely, to a time when the successors of Solomon

might be independant of either power; when "Israel should be the third with Egypt and with Assyria" (chap. xix. 24). Upon this act of King Hoshea the Assyrians overran Samaria, and the Egyptian alliance was broken.

This made Tirhakah king of Cush, who was evidently ruling over Egypt, or at any rate over Lower Egypt, threaten to invade Palestine in his turn; but he does not appear to have performed this threat, and it was not till the last year of the reign of Josiah (B.C. 609), that the kings of Egypt attempted to recover their lost influence over Palestine, when Pharaoh Nechoh (2 Kings, xxiii.) marched directly towards the Euphrates against Assyria, but was met by Josiah king of Judah, who was defeated at Megiddo (lat. 32° 24'), and slain in the battle. The Jews then made Jehoahaz king in place of his father. But Pharaoh Nechoh dethroned him after a short reign of three months, taking him prisoner at Riblah in the land of Hamath (lat. 32° 58'), and made his elder brother, Eliakim, king, who then changed his name to Jehoiakim. Nechoh required and received from him a tribute of an hundred talents of silver and one of gold. But the Egyptian influence over Judah soon ended, for, in the fourth year of the reign of Jehoiakim (B.C. 604, Jeremiah, xlvi.), Nebuchadnezzar marched against Judea and its allies, defeated Pharaoh Nechoh, and retook from the Egyptians Arabia Petræa, and all that belonged to them between the Euphrates and the river of Egypt [the valley of the Nile] (2 Kings, xxiv.)

Zedekiah, the next king of Judah, when he rebelled against Nebuchadnezzar, made an alliance with Pharaoh Hophra, and looked to him for assistance; and, indeed, when Nebuchadnezzar besieged Jerusalem, on the march of the Egyptian army, the Chaldees raised the siege (Jeremiah, xxxvii. 5) and withdrew the army; but this was the last time that the Egyptian power was able so to serve the Jews. The Assyrian party in the state, indeed, was in the minority, though assisted by the influence and eloquence of Jeremiah and Ezekiel, who warned their countrymen that trusting to the Egyptian alliance, against the power of Assyria, was leaning on a broken reed (Ezekiel, xxix. 6). But this advice had not been followed; the humiliating tribute to Assyria had been refused; their Egyptian allies were neither near enough, nor strong enough, to support them; they were soon entirely conquered and their nobles led captive to Babylon, and in less than a century afterwards, Egypt was made a province of the same country.

The Nile is never mentioned by name in our translation of the Old Testament; it is always called the river of Egypt, although the word Nile occurs in the original, נחל (Isaiah, xxvii. 12; Joshua, xv. 4, 47; 2 Kings, xxiv. 7), and perhaps in other places. In these places the river of Egypt, literally the Nile of the Egyptians, is spoken of as the boundary of Palestine. The desert appears to have been the natural boundary between Palestine and Egypt, and to fit these passages map-makers have created a stream in the desert, and called it Egyptus. But there is no difficulty in understanding the claim of the Jewish writers to extend Palestine to the valley of the Nile, to the Pelusian mouth, when we recollect that Solomon had ports on the Red Sea.

HERODOTUS.

THE earliest kings mentioned in the Egyptian traditions were their gods Osiris, Horus, and Typhon; these, however, they placed in a very remote antiquity, and showed three hundred and forty-five wooden statues of priests, no doubt royal priests or kings, who had all descended from father to son in a male line through that number of generations, since which they considered that no gods had been upon earth. The expression of Herodotus that "each was a Piromis born of a Piromis," may be quoted as a proof of the accuracy of his report, though the word *piromi*, which he thought meant *of good birth*, is, in the language of the Coptic version of the Scriptures, *a man*; and the meaning of his informer was that "each was a man born of a man."

The first man who reigned in Egypt was Menes. We are told that he built the city of Memphis and a celebrated temple of Vulcan; turned the river into a new channel, and raised a dyke to prevent its overflowing. He was followed by three hundred and thirty kings, including one queen, Nitocris, and eighteen Ethiopians. The names of all these were told to Herodotus, but the only one whose name and actions [in connection with Memphis] were worth recording, was

Mœris, who built the vestibule to the north front of the temple of Vulcan, and dug the lake of that name: he lived about nine hundred years before the time of Herodotus. These were succeeded by

Sesostris. He was a great warrior, conquering with his fleets the nations on the shores of the Red Sea, and with his armies Palestine, Scythia, Thrace, Ethiopia, and the neighbouring countries. He was the only Egyptian monarch who reigned over Ethiopia. By means of his captives he formed the trenches by which Egypt is everywhere intersected and irrigated. He is also said to have altered the tenure of the soil, parcelling it out in square lots of equal size, one to each man, for which they paid an annual rent to the king. The priests and soldiers were exempted from this tax; and though the military lost this exemption in the reign of Sethon, they must have regained it at an after time, as they possessed it in common with the priests in the time of Herodotus.

Of his son Phero, who succeeded him, we are only told that he was not warlike, but erected two obelisks at the temple of the Sun [at Thebes or at Heliopolis], each of a single stone, and each an hundred cubits in length and eight in breadth. We are not told what city was the residence of these kings; and it seems probable that Herodotus mistook his title Pharaoh for his name.

The next, called Proteus in the language of the Greeks, was of Memphis. His sanctuary was standing there in the time of Herodotus, and he was said by the priest to have lived at the time of the Trojan war.

Rampsinitus followed, also of Memphis. He built the western portico of the temple of Vulcan, and set up in front of it two statues twenty-five cubits in height, called Summer and Winter. He amassed an amount of riches which none of his successors could equal. At his death the good government and prosperity of Egypt ceased for some time. The three following kings seem to have been of Sais. The first was

Cheops, who closed the temples, forbade sacrifices, and made all the people of Egypt work at his pyramid, and at roads along which the stones were brought, a work as great as the pyramid itself. These were brought from the Arabian quarries to the Nile, transported across the river in barges, and carried thence along the road to the Libyan mountains. This oppressive work lasted twenty years. The pyramid is square, each side measuring eight hundred feet, and no stone less than thirty feet; it was built in steps, and then finished downwards from the top, smoothing off the steps. His daughter built a smaller pyramid, measuring one hundred and fifty feet each way.

His brother Chephren succeeded to him, and continued his tyranny. He built a pyramid seven hundred and sixty feet on each side, faced with marble on the first range, but containing no chambers within it. These two kings together reigned one hundred and six years; and, to avoid the mention of their hateful names, the pyramids are named after the shepherd Philitis, who fed his herds in that region.

Mycerinus, the son of Cheops, succeeded: he opened the temples; was a mild ruler and just judge.

Asychis reigned after him, probably at Memphis, as he built the eastern portico to the temple of Vulcan. He erected the largest pyramid, which is of bricks made of clay.

Then followed Anysis, a blind king, of the city of that name. He was dethroned by

Sabacon, an Ethiopian who invaded Egypt with his army, and reigned fifty years.

A priest of Vulcan named Sethon reigned next. He illused the military order, and took away from them the allotment of twelve acres for each man, which they held under former kings. During this reign Egypt was invaded by Sanacharib, king of the Arabians and Syrians. There had been three hundred and forty-one generations between the first king and this; and within this period the sun had four times risen contrary to his common course—twice he had risen where he now sets, and twice set where he now rises.

On the death of Sethon the priest of Vulcan, the Egyptians became free: the country was divided into twelve parts, each under a separate king. These kings built the labyrinth in common, a little below the lake Mœris, and nearly opposite to the city of Crocodiles. It was a work surpassing the pyramids, consisting of twelve roofed halls within one outer wall, and as many more subterranean halls under the former, containing together three thousand chambers, intended as sepulchres of the kings and sacred crocodiles.

One of these twelve kings was Psammitichus, who when young had fled into Syria from Sabacon the Ethiopian, who had put to death his father Necho. He then reigned over the Saitic district, as one of these twelve, till expelled by the jealousy of his colleagues; but afterwards, by the help of some Ionian and Carian auxiliaries, he overcame the others, and made himself master of all Egypt. He added the south portico to the temple of Vulcan at Memphis, and opposite to it a hall for Apis, surrounded with a colonnade of colossal figures twelve cubits high. To the Ionians and Carians he allotted lands, where they and their descendants dwelt, a little below Bubastis, on the Pelusian mouth of the Nile. He reigned fifty-four years, twenty-nine of which were spent in besieging Azotus, a city of Syria.

Necho succeeded him: he began the canal from the Nile above Bubastis to the Red Sea near Patumus, an Arabian town; but he left this unfinished, and invaded the Syrians, overthrowing them at Magdolus, and taking Kadytis, a city of Syria. He was succeeded by his son Psammis.

Psammis made an expedition against Ethiopia, and reigned six years.

His son Apries enjoyed a prosperity nearly equal to that of Psammitichus, during the first twenty-five years of his reign. He led with success an army against Sidon, and a fleet against Tyre: but his army, when defeated in the expedition against the Cyrenæans, revolted against their king, and set up Amasis. The Carians and Ionians remained faithful to Apries at Sais, but he was defeated by Amasis and the native troops, and put to death.

Amasis now reigned at Sais. He was of low birth, of the city of Siuph. At Sais he built a portico to the temple of Minerva, ornamented with colossal statues, and androsphinxes: some of the stones were brought from Memphis, and some from Elephantine. At Memphis he built the beautiful temple of Isis, and made a supine colossal figure seventy feet long in front of the temple of Vulcan; and a similar statue at Sais. Under him Egypt enjoyed an unexampled prosperity. He gave up the city of Naucratis to the Greek colonists. He conquered Cyprus, and made the people pay tribute. He reigned forty-four years, and died just before the Persian invasion under Cambyses.

Psammenitus, the son of Amasis, encamped at the Pelusian mouth of the Nile, waiting the approach of Cambyses, who had got leave of the Arabians to march through their territory and who was joined by Phanes, one of the Greek colonists in Egypt; the rest of the Greeks fought on the side of the Egyptians. The Persians were successful. Herodotus adds that, when he was upon the spot, he could distinguish the strong skulls of the shaved Egyptians from the weak skulls of the turbaned Persians.

Cambyses soon after took Memphis and Sais, deposing Psammenitus; his army afterwards entered Thebes. His expedition, however, against the Ethiopians failed for want of provisions; and a detachment of fifty thousand, sent against the Ammonians to an oasis seven days' march from Thebes, called the islands of the Happy, after passing by the oasis, perished in the desert. He slew with his own hand Apis, the sacred bull at Memphis, in derision of the Egyptian prejudices. On this conquest, the history of Egypt was sunk in the history of Persia.

Cambyses entered Egypt by the coast of the Mediterranean, which Herodotus considered the military way; but we shall hereafter see that Strabo thought the more circuitous route by the coasts of the Red Sea the best. He marched from Phœnicia through the land of the Palæstines [Philistines] to the neighbourhood of Kadytis, a city about the size of Sardis; thence by the coast through Arabia to Jenysus; thence to the lake Serbonis in Egypt. Kadytis is evidently to the south of the Philistines, and is probably Kadesh-Barnea (lat. 31° 20'), and must not be confounded with Kadytis, the city which was taken by Necho. It has been usual to consider the latter Kadytis as Jerusalem; but a reference to the map, and to 2 Kings, xxiii., will make this very improbable. Necho marched towards the Euphrates [through Palestine northward], defeated the Jews at Megiddo [lat. 32° 24'; Herodotus calls it Magdolus], took Jehoahaz prisoner at Riblah (lat. 32° 58'), and then [according to Herodotus] took Kadytis [probably Kadesh; lat. 32° 55'], a city of Syria. If Necho had taken Jerusalem, it would no doubt have been mentioned by the Jewish historians.

" The medical art is thus distributed by the Egyptians: every disease has a physician to itself, who cures nothing else; all places are filled, therefore, with medical practitioners; for there are doctors for the eyes, doctors of the head, and doctors of the teeth, and of the stomach, and of all inward complaints. Their lamentations and funerals are conducted in the following manner. On the demise of a man of respectability, all the females of the household cover their heads, and even their faces, with mud; and then, leaving the corpse at home, traverse the city lamenting, with their loins girt and their bosoms bare. With them follow all the relatives; the men lament by themselves; they also are girded. This done, they carry the dead to be embalmed. There are certain persons who practice this art. These, when they receive the corpse, exhibit to the persons bringing it wooden models of bodies, painted to resemblance, as patterns. The most elaborate of these models represent, they say, him whose name on this occasion I do not think it lawful to mention. The second model is of an inferior kind, and cheaper, and the third is still less costly. These models being set forth, the embalmer asks to which pattern they will have the dead prepared. The relatives agreeing as to the price to be paid, depart. The embalmers then proceed at their own home with their work, as follows: if the most costly method is to be practised, in the first place, with an iron hook they extract the brains by the nose, and what then remains by means of drugs injected. Then, with a sharp Ethiopian stone, they open the body, from which they remove all the contents, and having cleansed them, and suffused palm wine, they inject pounded aromatics. Then, filling the cavity with pure bruised myrrh and cassia, and other aromatics, excepting frankincense, they sew it up, and afterwards salt it in nitre, in which it lies seventy days; longer is not permitted. This time elapsed, the body is washed, and then bound about with bandages of fine linen bespread with gum, which the Egyptians in most things use instead of glue. The relatives having received the body thus prepared, enclose it in a wooden case, which they make in the resemblance of the human form. When so enclosed, they consign it as a treasure to the family sepulchre, placing it erect against the wall. This is the most costly mode of preserving the dead.

" Those who, to avoid expense, choose the middle mode, have their relatives embalmed in the following manner: the body, instead of being opened and embowelled, is filled with an oil drawn from the cedar, and then steeped the allotted time in nitre; after which the injection, by its efficacy, clears the cavity of its contents, while the nitre has dissolved the flesh, leaving to the corpse only the skin and bones. This done, they deliver it to the relatives, without bestowing upon it further pains. The third method of embalming, practised only for the most indigent, consists in cleansing the body with drugs, and corning it seventy days; after which it is delivered to those who remove it."—Taylor's Translation.

Herodotus repeatedly omits the name of one of the gods as too sacred to be mentioned. Dr. Young conjectures, I know not upon what authority, that it was Osiris; but Plutarch (*De Iside et Osiride*) quotes Hecatœus of Abdera for the fact that Ammon was a name not to be uttered.

The Egyptians deem a hog a foul animal, and therefore if any one in passing does but touch this animal with his garments, he goes instantly to the river and washes.

The Nile was navigated in large barges of many thousand talents burden: these could sail against the stream when the wind was directly favorable, at other times they were towed from the banks. They came down the river by the force of the stream, and, as a vessel will only obey the rudder when going *through* the water, but not when floating with the stream, they adopted the plan practised by Captain Hall in descending the river Guayaquil in the year 1821, of trailing a weight along the bottom of the river, after the vessel, whereby its progress is made to differ from that of the stream, by which means it is made obedient to the rudder.—See Basil Hall's South America.

Herodotus learned at Chemmis that Danaus, who migrated to Greece, was a native of that city. He understood that Thon, who received Menelaus (Odyssey, iv.) was warden of the mouth of the Nile, under Proteus, who reigned at Memphis. He attributes to Sesostris what we learn from Genesis took place at a much earlier time, namely the making all the land, except that held by the two privileged classes, pay a fifth of its produce as rent to the crown. His mistake, in reporting that the largest pyramid is of brick, is unpardonable. He says that he had visited Thebes, and that in writing the history of Egypt he meant the country below Elephantine, which was watered by the Nile. But, notwithstanding this, it is pretty evident that he got his information chiefly from the Greek colonists in the Delta and the priests of Vulcan at Memphis; and that his history is that of Lower Egypt, which was reigned over sometimes by independent kings at Memphis or Sais, and sometimes by the sovereigns of all Egypt. The Ionian colonists on the coast asserted that the name of Egypt belonged to the Delta, and the rest of the country they called part Libya part Arabia.

If we examine the chronology of these kings of Memphis, who succeeded one another without interval, allowing twenty-two years and a half for each reign of which the length is not mentioned, and considering B.C. 525 as the date of the Persian invasion, it will stand thus:

B.C. 1330   Mœris (900 years before Herodotus).
    983   Sesostris, the conqueror of Palestine.
            Phero, his son.
    938   Proteus (the Trojan War).
            Rampsinitus.
    893   Cheops, Chephren, } together reigned 106 years.
    787   Mycerinus, son of Cheops.
            Asychis.
            Anysis, dethroned when blind, and probably old, by Sabbacon, at the beginning of his reign.
    720   Sabbacon, the Ethiopian conqueror, who reigned 50 years. Necho, also put to death by Sabbacon.

B.C. 670   Psammeticus, the son of Necho, reigned 54 years.
    616   Necho II., reigned 16 years.
    600   Psammis, reigned 6 years.
    594   Apries, reigned 25 years.
    569   Amasis, reigned 44 years.
    525   Cambyses conquered Egypt.

Now if we compare these dates with the known dates in the chronological table, we shall find Sesostris the conqueror of Palestine coincide with Shishak the conqueror of Palestine, of 2 Chron. xii.; Necho II. coincide with Pharaoh Nechoh, of 2 Kings, xxiii.; Apries with Pharaoh Hophra, of Jeremiah, xliv.

The Trojan War falls to the time assigned to it by Newton. The assertion that none of the three hundred and thirty predecessors of Sesostris did anything worth recording, must be understood as relating to the history of Memphis and Lower Egypt, in which sense it was no doubt true: they had all resided at a distance, and had left it unornamented with temples and other public buildings.

In the case of the son of Sesostris, Herodotus seems to have mistaken his title Pharaoh for his proper name. Rampsinitus was no doubt one of the last of the family of Rameses.

DIODORUS SICULUS.

ACCORDING to the sacred books which were written by the priests, containing an account of the magnificence and deeds of their kings, Egypt had been reigned over by

    4   Ethiopians, for about -   36 years.
        Persians, for about   - - 135 years.
        Macedonians, for about   276 years.

470 Native Egyptian kings.
5 Native Egyptian queens.

Menas was the first man who succeeded the gods on the throne.

Gnefactus followed after some time; he had fifty-two successors of this line. Then came

Busiris and seven successors, and then another

Busiris, who built Thebes, celebrated for its porticoes.

Osymandyas was one of the greatest contributors to the buildings of Thebes: his library and tomb were very splendid: we are not told when he reigned.

Uchureus, the eighth from Osymandyas, built Memphis, which was so well placed for importance and strength between the lake and the river that the following kings left Thebes and built their palaces here. The splendour of Memphis continued till the rise of Alexandria.

Mœris, the twelfth after Egyptus, built the portico on the north side of Memphis. He made a canal of five leagues in length from the Nile to the lake Mœris, with sluices, as a reservoir to regulate the inundation of the Nile. He built two pyramids.

Sesoosis, the seventh from Mœris, was greater than any of his predecessors: he conquered Arabia and Libya. His army consisted of six hundred thousand foot, twenty-four thousand horse, twenty-eight thousand chariots. He afterwards conquered Ethiopia, India beyond the Ganges, Scythia, and Thrace, and fixed the yearly tributes which the conquered nations should pay. He made two obelisks of hard stone, each one hundred and twenty cubits high, on which he described the greatness of the kingdom, and the tributes of the subject states. He reigned 33 years.

Sesoosis, his son, succeeded.

Amasis followed, after some generations; in whose reign Actisanes, king of Ethiopia, successfully invaded Egypt, and governed it well: at his death

Mendes, or Marros, a native prince, succeeded: he built the Labyrinth.

Ketna, whom the Greeks called Proteus, succeeded, after five generations: in his time was the Trojan War.

His son and successor was solely employed in heaping up wealth. Nileus then succeeded.

Chemmis, the eighth after Proteus, reigned 50 years in Memphis, and built the greatest of the three pyramids.

Cephren, his brother, or Chabryis, his son, succeeded; who reigned 56 years, and built the second pyramid.

Mycerinus, or Cherinus, the son of Chemmis, succeeded: he began the third pyramid, but died before it was finished; he put his name on the north side of it. But some authors assign the pyramids to other kings.

Bocchoris, surnamed the wise, a great lawgiver, succeeded; and then Sabbacon, the Ethiopian, governed very well for some time, till he voluntarily retired to Ethiopia.

Egypt was then governed for fifteen years by a council of twelve that sat at Memphis, till one of the twelve, Psammitichus of Sais, by the help of Arabian, Carian, and Ionian mercenaries, made himself king of all Egypt.

Apries succeeded, after four generations: he invaded Phenicia, and conquered Sidon, and reigned 22 years.

Amasis rebelled against him, and eventually succeeded: he reigned for 55 years, and died at the time that

Cambyses, the Persian, conquered Egypt, in the third year of the sixty-third Olympiad.

The kings of Egypt were not like other kings, whose will is law, but they obeyed the law in every thing they did: they gained the love and obedience of their subjects, conquered foreign countries, and enriched and beautified their own. The priests were called to assist the king with their counsel, and the blame of what was done wrong was laid, not upon the king, but upon the counsellors who advised him.

The revenue of the kingdom was divided into three parts; one part for the priests, one for the king, and one for the military order.

The Court of Justice consisted of thirty judges, of whom one was the president; they were maintained by the king, and decided according to the eight books of the laws. These judges were the best men chosen from the most considerable cities; ten from Thebes, ten from Memphis, ten from Heliopolis. The whole of the proceedings were in writing.

The priests married only one wife; other persons, as many as they chose; and there was no such thing as illegitimacy, every one being held to be the legitimate child of his father.

The year was divided into twelve months of thirty days each, and five days and a quarter over, without any intercalation.

" After the embalming, when a body is to be finally buried, the relations fix a day, and send for the forty-two judges and all the friends of the deceased, saying that he is about to pass the lake. The judges sit in a semicircle, and a boat is brought, conducted by a boatman called in Egyptian, Charon; and, before the body is put into the boat, any one may bring forward his accusation against the deceased, and, if he shows that he has led a wicked life, the judges declare accordingly, and he loses the usual burial: but if the accuser fails he is punished. The relations then praise the deceased, not for his rank, for all Egyptians are equally noble, but for his virtues, and pray the infernal gods to admit him into the company of the pious. The body is then placed in the family catacombs. They sometimes deposited the bodies of their ancestors as pledges for loans of money, and were subject to heavy disgrace if they did not redeem them."

The statuaries cut their statues by mathematical rules, while the Greeks judged the symmetry of a figure by the sight of the whole.

The Delta was the most fertile part of Egypt: it was watered not only by the rise of the Nile, but they raised the water by means of an engine, invented by Archimedes, called from its form the cochlea. The rise of the Nile was measured by a nilometer at Memphis, and information sent to all the towns how many feet the water had risen, and also at what time it began to abate.

The approach to Egypt from Syria is made difficult by the Servonian bog called the Barathron, over which men cannot walk; it is narrow, but thirty-six miles long, and surrounded by sand hills. The only port between Paratonium in Libya, and Joppa in Syria, is that of Pharos.

The Ethiopians boast that the Egyptians were a colony from them, and that they owed to them their laws, civilization, letters, and religion; that hieroglyphics, which in Egypt were confined to the priests, were in Ethiopia the letters of the people. The priests of both nations wear a high crown with a ball on the top, wreathed with serpents called asps, and carry a ploughshare for a sceptre. They elect a king from among the order of priests, who rules according to the ancient laws of the kingdom. The interior of Arabia is inhabited by herdsmen who live in tents.

The Court of Justice mentioned above approached very nearly to a representative chamber; we must not understand that the three cities, but the three districts, of Upper, Middle, and Lower Egypt, elected ten judges each.

The account of the trial of the deceased, which takes place at the ceremony of burial, is remarkably confirmed by the pictures of the last judgement, which are found at the end of the manuscripts on papyrus, discovered in the mummies.

In one of these, an hieratic manuscript, the property of Lord Mountnorris, published in the Hieroglyphical Collections of the Egyptian Society, Osiris is seated on a throne with his usual sceptres, the whip in his right hand and hook in his left, and a serpent or asp hanging from each shoulder; before him is another sceptre, and a female wolf, and on a shelf four small gods or statues, with the heads of a man, a mastiff, a greyhound, and a hawk, respectively. Near him stands the god Thoth, with the head of an Ibis, writing with style and tablet, probably the actions of the deceased. On the ground stands a tall pair of scales, with a little genius sitting on the top of the support; under each arm of the beam stands a god, with greyhound and hawk heads, probably, by comparison with a tablet in the same volume, where the names are written, Anubis and Pthah-sokar Osiris; these two are adjusting the scales. Behind stands the deceased with his name over him, followed by the characters Nos. 26 and 39 of Plate V., " a man deceased"; his clothing is a petticoat from his hips to his ankles, suspended by a brace over the right shoulder; he is between two goddesses. In many pictures we have also the forty-two assessors mentioned above.

The high crown or cap with a ball on the top, worn by the Ethiopian priests, is the crown of Upper Egypt; see the Tablet of Abydos, Plate III., where the crowns of Upper and Lower Egypt occur alternately under the ovals. The ploughshare for a sceptre is in the hand of many gods in the Egyptian sculptures; it may be seen in Plate V. fig. 14, where it is the letter M.

Diodorus is evidently more correct than Herodotus when he says that Mœris made the lake available for irrigation, not that he dug it.

Of the early kings mentioned by Diodorus we can make very little. Menas is in all the lists the first man who reigned upon earth: Osymandyas was not a fabulous person, though we may not be able to identify him; I should conjecture the name intended was Oseimen-pthah.

If we count backwards from Cambyses, we shall find that Diodorus places the Trojan war two reigns and seven generations earlier than Herodotus does; hence, allowing twenty-two years and a half for the length of a reign, and thirty-nine years for a generation, which we shall hereafter see is the average length, we must suppose him to have placed the Trojan war about B.C. 1200. Six generations before the Trojan war reigned Amasis, that is B.C. 1430, whom we shall hereafter recognize in Manetho's list of kings as reigning at that time; and some generations before him lived Sesoosis, the fabulous hero, who, like the god Osiris himself, conquered India beyond the Ganges, whom we shall recognize in Manetho as living about B.C. 1600, but who agrees with the Sesostris of Herodotus in nothing but in name.

The two historians may be thus compared:

HERODOTUS.	DIODORUS SICULUS.
	Sesoosis (about B.C. 1600), the conqueror of India beyond the Ganges.
	Sesoosis, his son.
	(Several generations.)
Mœris (B.C. 1330).	Amasis (B.C. 1430).

F

	(Six generations.)
Sesostris (B.C. 985), the conqueror of Palestine and Thrace.	Proteus or Ketna. The Trojan war. (B.C. 1200).
Phero, his son.	Remphis, his son.
Proteus. Trojan war (B.C. 940).	(Seven generations.)
Rampsinitus.	Nileus.
Cheops.	Chemmis.
Chephren.	Cephren.
Mycerinus.	Myserinus.
Asychis.	Bocchoris (at Sais).
Anysis (Memphis).	Sabbacon.
Sabbacon.	Psammiticus.
Psammiticus.	
Necho II.	(Four reigns.)
Psammis.	
Apries.	Apries.
Amasis.	Amasis.
Cambyses.	Cambyses.

MANETHO.

MANETHO's history of Egypt exists only as quotations in the works of more modern authors, several of whom have preserved his list of kings, and one, *viz.* Josephus, has preserved more particular accounts of those parts of his work which related to the Jews. These different fragments occasionally differ in the length of reigns and mode of spelling the names. Manetho was an Egyptian priest, who lived under Ptolemy Philadelphus. He had read Herodotus's history.

1st Dynasty,—Of the City of This.

1. Menes: he reigned 7, 17, 30, or 62 years, and was killed by a hippopotamus.
2. Athothis, his son, reigned 27 or 57 years: he built the palace at Memphis, where he practised medicine, and wrote upon anatomy.
3. Cencenes, his son, reigned 31 or 39 years.
4. Venephes, Enephes, or Venephres, his son, reigned 23 or 42 years: in his reign there was a great plague or famine in Egypt: he built the pyramids near the city Choe, Cochome, or Chovone.
5. Usaphœdus, or Usaphaes, his son, reigned 20 years.
6. Miebidus, or Niebes, his son, reigned 26 years.
7. Semempses, or Mempses, his son, reigned 18 years: there was a pestilence in his reign.
8. Bienaches, or Ubienthes, his son, reigned 26 years.

Together, 252 or 253 or 213 years.

2d Dynasty,—Of This.

1. Bœthus, or Bochus, reigned 38 years: during his reign there was a chasm in the earth near Bubastus, and many persons perished.
2. Cœechus, reigned 39 years: under him the bulls Apis in Memphis and Mnevis in Heliopolis, and the goat at Mendes, were made gods.
3. Binothris, or Biophis, reigned 47 years; in his reign it was determined that women might succeed to the throne.
4. Tlas, reigned 17 years.
5. Sethenes, 41 years.
6. Chœres, 17 years; during which reigns nothing happened worth mentioning.
7. Nephercheres, 25 years: in his time the waters of the Nile were mixed with honey during eleven days.
8. Sesochris, 48 years: his

height was five cubits, and his breadth three.

9. Cheneres, 30 years.

Together, 302 or 297 years.

3d Dynasty,—*Of Memphis.*

1. Necherophes, reigned 28 years: in his reign the Lybians revolted from the Egyptians, but submitted through fright at an unusual increase of the moon.

2. Tosorthrus, or Sesorthus, 29 years: he is called Asclepius by the Egyptians, on account of his medical knowledge; he first built with hewn stones.

3. Tyris, reigned 7 years.
4. Mesochris, 17 years.
5. Soyphis, 16 years.
6. Tosertasis, 19 years.
7. Aches, 42 years.
8. Sephuris, 30 years.
9. Cerpheres, 26 years; but these six did nothing worth the mention.

Together, 197 or 214 years.

4th Dynasty,—*Of Memphis, but of a different family.*

1. Soris, reigned 29 years.
2. Suphis, 63 years.
3. Suphis, 66 years: one of these two kings built the pyramid which Herodotus says was built by Cheops: he was arrogant towards the gods, but when penitent wrote the sacred book which the Egyptians value so highly. Of the following kings nothing is known.

4. Mencheres, 63 years.
5. Rhatœres, 25 years.
6. Bicheris, 22 years.
7. Seberscheres, 7 years.
8. Thampthis, 9 years.

Together, 284 or 448 years.

5th Dynasty,—*Of Elephantine.*

1. Usercheres, reigned 28 yrs.
2. Sephres, 13 years.

3. Nephercheres, 20 years.
4. Sisires, 7 years.
5. Cheres, 20 years.
6. Rathures, 44 years.
7. Mencheres, 9 years.
8. Tancheres, 44 years.
9. Abnus, 33 years.

Together, 248 years.

6th *Dynasty,—Of Memphis.*

1. Othoes, was killed by his guards after a reign of 30 years.
2. Phius, reigned 53 years.
3. Methusuphis, 7 years.
4. Phiops, began to reign at six years old, and reigned till he was an hundred.
5. Menthesuphis, reigned 1 year.
6. Queen Nitocris, reigned 12 years: she was handsome among women, and brave among men; some say that she built the third pyramid.

7th *Dynasty,—Of Memphis.*

5 or 70 kings, who together reigned 70 days or 75 years.

8th *Dynasty,—Of Memphis.*

5 or 27 kings, who together reigned 100 or 146 years.

9th *Dynasty,—Of Heracleopolis.*

1. Achthoes, who was worse than all his predecessors, and committed such crimes that he became mad, and was killed by a crocodile.

3 or 18 other kings.

Together, 100 or 409 years.

10th *Dynasty,—Of Heracleopolis.*

19 kings, who reigned 185 years.

11th Dynasty,—Of Diospolis.

15 kings, who reigned 27 years.

16 Amenemes, who reigned 16 years.

So far the first book of Manetho, including 192 kings, and 2300 years.

12th Dynasty,—Of Diospolis.

1. Sesonchosis, or Geson Gosis, son of Amenemes, reigned 46 years.

2. Ammenemes, reigned 38 years, and was slain by his own eunuchs.

3. Sesostris, reigned 48 years. He conquered all Asia in 9 years and Europe as far as Thrace, erecting monuments of his conquest in those countries: by the Egyptians he is thought to be the first after Osiris.

4. Lachares, or Labares, reigned 8 years: he built the Labyrinth in Arsenoites, as a tomb for himself.

5. Ammeres, 8 years.

6. Ammenemes, 8 years.

7. Scemiophris, his sister, 4 yrs.

Together, 160 or 245 years.

13th Dynasty,—Of Diospolis.

60 kings, reigned 184 or 453 years.

14th Dynasty,—Of Xois.

76 kings, reigned 184 or 484 years.

15th Dynasty,—Of the Phenician Shepherd Kings.

In the reign of King Timœus there came up from the east men of an ignoble race, who had the confidence to invade our country and easily subdued it without a battle, burning the cities, demolishing the temples, slaying the men, and reducing the women and children to slavery. They made

1. Salatis, one of themselves, king: he reigned at Memphis, and made the Upper and Lower region [of Egypt] tributary; garrisoned fit places particularly on the eastern frontier, through fear the Assyrians should invade the country. He rebuilt and strongly fortified the city of Abaris in the Sethroite Nome, [that is, near Bubastus] and garrisoned it with 250,000 men, as a treasure city. He reigned 19 years.

2. Beon, reigned 44 years.
3. Pachan, or Apachnas, 61 or 36 years.
4. Staan, or Janias, 50 years.
5. Archles, or Assis, 49 years.
6. Apophis, or Aphobis, 61 years.

Together, 284 years: it was in this period that Joseph ruled in Egypt.

16th *Dynasty,—Of Hellenic Shepherd Kings.*

32 kings, reigned 518 years.

17th *Dynasty,—Of Diospolis.*

43 shepherd kings and 43 Theban kings at Diospolis, reigned for 151 years.

All this nation was called Hycsōs, or Shepherd kings; for the first syllable, Hyc, in the sacred dialect, means *a king*, and Sos, in the vulgar tongue, *a shepherd*: some say they were Arabs. These shepherd kings and their descendants retained possession of Egypt for 511 years.

18th *Dynasty,—Of Diospolis.*

After this the kings of the Thebaid and the other [*i.e.* Lower] Egypt rose against the shepherds, and after a long war Alisphragmuthosis drove the shepherds, or captives as they were sometimes called, out of the other parts of Egypt, and confined them in the district of Abaris, which they strongly fortified to protect their property.

1. Amosis, or Tethmosis, or Thummosis, his son, besieged them in their strong hold with 480,000 men, reduced them to capitulate, and they left Egypt in number 240,000, and marched through the desert towards Syria, and built the city of Jerusalem, in the country now called Judea, which they fortified against the Assyrians. He reigned 25 years.
2. Chebros, his son, 13 years.
3. Amenophis, 20 or 24 years.
4. His sister Amensis, or Amesses, 22 years.
5. Misaphris, or Mephres, 13 years.
6. Misphragmuthosis, 26 yrs: in whose time the deluge of Deucalion happened.
7. Tuthmosis, 9 years.
8. Amenophis, 31: he is considered as the Memnon to whom the musical statue was erected.
9. Horus, 37 years.
10. His daughter Acenchres, or Acherres, 12 or 32 years.
11. Her brother Rathos, 6 or 9 years.
12. Chebres, or Acencheres, 12 years.
13. Acencheres, or Acherres, 12 years.
14. Armeses, or Armais, 5 years; called also Danaus; who, being driven out by his brother Egyptus, settled in Argos.
15. Ramesses, or Egyptus, 1 year, or 48 years.

Armesses, the son of Miammous, 66 years. This king seems to be the same as the last, and Miammous the same as Armais No. 14; not being in the list, but inserted in a quotation in Josephus as the last but one of this dynasty.

16. Amenophis, 19 years.

In all 348 or 263 years.

This last king, or one of his immediate predecessors, being warned by the priests to cleanse the whole country of lepers and unclean persons, gathered them together, and sent them, to the number of 80,000, to work at the quarries on the east side of the Nile. And there were amongst them some learned priests equally affected with leprosy. When they had been some time in that miserable state, the king set apart for them the city Avaris, which had been left empty by the Shepherds, and which, according to the sacred writings, is a Typhonian city. When they had possession of the city they revolted, and made Osarsiph, a priest of Heliopolis, their ruler, who afterwards changed his name to Moses. He made many laws, directly opposed to the customs of the Egyptians, forbidding them to worship their gods and sacred animals. He sent ambassadors to Jerusalem, to the Shepherds whom Tethmosis had driven out, who gladly sent 200,000 men to their assistance, in hopes of regaining the dominion of Egypt. Amenoph at first retreated to Ethiopia, whose king was his friend; but, returning with a great force, slew many of the Shepherds, and pursued the rest into Syria.

20th *Dynasty,—Of Diospolis.*

7 or 12 kings, who reigned 135 or 172 years.

21st *Dynasty,—Of Tanis.*

1. Smendes, 26 years.
2. Psusennes, 46 years.
3. Nephelcheres, 4 years.
4. Amenophthis, 9 years.
5. Osochor, 6 years.
6. Psinaches, 9 years.
7. Psusennes, 14 years.

Together, 130 years.

22d *Dynasty,—Of Bubastus.*

1. Sesonchis, 21 years.
2. Osorthon, 15 years.
3, 4, and 5, reigned 25 years.
6. Tacellothis, 13 years.
7, 8, and 9, reigned 42 years.

Together, 120 years.

23d Dynasty,—Of Tanis.

1. Petubastes, reigned 40 yrs.: and in his time the Olympiads began.
2. Osorchon, whom the Egyptians called Hercules, reigned 8 years.
3. Psammus, 10 years.
4. Zeet, 31 years.

Together, 28 or 44 years.

24th Dynasty,—Of Sais.

1. Bocchoris, reigned 6 years.

25th Dynasty,—Of Ethiopians.

1. Sabacon, having conquered Bocchoris, burnt him alive, and reigned over Egypt 8 years.
2. Sevechus his son, 14 years.
3. Taracus, 18 years.

Together, 40 or 44 years.

26th Dynasty,—Of Sais.

1. Ammeres, an Ethiopian, 18 years.
2. Stephinathis, 7 years.
3. Nechepsus, 6 years.
4. Nechao, 6 or 8 years.
5. Psammetichus, 44 or 54 yrs.
6. Nechao II., who took Jerusalem, and led Joachaz, the king, prisoner to Egypt, reigned 6 yrs.
7. Psammuthes, or Psammetichus II., 17 years.
8. Vaphris, 19 or 25 years; to whom the Jews fled, when the Assyrians took Jerusalem.
9. Amosis, 42 or 44 years.
10. Psammecherites, 6 mths.

Together, 147 or 150 years.

27th Dynasty,—Of Persians.

1. Cambyses reigned over his own kingdom, Persia, 5 years, and then over Egypt 1 year.
2. The Magi, 7 months.

MANETHO. 43

3. Darius, the son of Hystaspes, 36 years.
4. Xerxes the Great, the son of Darius, 21 years.
5. Artabanus, 7 months.
6. Artaxerxes, 41 years.
7. Xerxes II., 2 months.
8. Sogdianus, 7 months.
9. Darius, the son of Xerxes, 19 years.

120 or 124 years in all.

28th *Dynasty,—Of Sais.*

Amyrtœus, 6 years.

29th *Dynasty,—Of Mendes.*

1. Nepherites, reigned 6 yrs.
2. Achoris, 13 years.
3. Psammuthes, 1 year.
4. Muthes, 1 year.
5. Nephorites, 4 months.

Together, 21 years.

30th *Dynasty,—Of Sebennytus.*

1. Nectanebes, 10 or 18 yrs.
2. Teos, 2 years.
3. Nectanebes, 8 or 18 years.

Together, 20 or 38 years.

31st *Dynasty.*

1. Ochus ruled Persia 20, and then Egypt 2 or 4 years.
2. Arses, his son, 3 or 4 years.
3. Darius, 4 or 6 years, whom
4. Alexander the Great overthrew and slew.

This third book of Manetho contains 1,050 years.

The internal and, as we shall hereafter see, external evidence prove that Manetho's history deserves our best attention, and make us wish that it had come down to us entire. It is very little more than a list of kings' names: we are not even told which of the dynasties succeeded one another, and which reigned at the same time in different parts of Egypt. This however we can partly learn from knowing that some of the kings reigned over both Upper and Lower Egypt, which was evidently not the case with others. For instance, when the kingdom of Thebes was so weak that it could not defend its southern frontier from its fierce and less civilized neighbours the Ethiopians, it could hardly have held Lower Egypt under its sway. So also when the Phenician or Canaanite Shepherds overran the lower region, there could have been no very powerful dynasty ruling at Tanis, or at Bubastus.

Of the dynasties before the Shepherd kings we have no certain means of forming an opinion, and therefore can do but little in the way of arrangement; but of the later dynasties the case does not seem hopeless. Manetho has given us a few dates, and contemporary history has given us a few more; and, however little weight we may give to these, at any rate we are certain that Manetho was too good a chronologist to put them down in a way to be inconsistent with one another.

The dates on which we must rest are the following:

B.C. 970 Shishak, or Sesonchis, of Bubastus flourished (2 Chronicles, xii.).
900 Thuoris of Thebes (Trojan War).
776 Petubastus of Tanis (first Olympiad).
729 Sevechus of Ethiopia (2 Kings, xvii.).
608 Nechao II. of Sais (2 Kings, xxiii.).
525 Cambyses of Persia.

There are two opinions respecting the time of the Trojan War, and I shall hereafter give my reasons for preferring the more modern date of B.C. 900. Manetho dates his kings also by means of Danaus and Deucalion, but as just the same doubt hangs over the time when these two Greeks lived, no further precision would be gained by referring to them.

If we put down Thuoris at B.C. 900, as the point from which we begin in the Diospolitan dynasties (see the Chart of History, Plate I.) and, taking the mean of the two accounts, allow five hundred and fifteen years for the length of the eighteenth and nineteenth dynasties, which is twenty-three years and a half for each reign, we shall find that Amosis and the expulsion of the Shepherd kings took place about B.C. 1415: and so in the other direction, allowing one hundred and fifty years for the twentieth dynasty, we shall find its end agree exactly with the Ethiopian invasion; and this coincidence goes far to prove that we have done right in supposing that Manetho meant about B.C. 900, for the time of the Trojan War.

In the same way with the Tanitic dynasties, the twenty-first and twenty-third; we find that the twenty-third dynasty ceased about fifty years after the beginning of the Olympiads, or B.C. 730, from which we deduce that though Sabbacon put down the expiring family of Rameses in Upper Egypt, the Tanitic kings preserved their throne till the reign of Sevechus, his more powerful successor. With the dynasties of Sais there is no difficulty; Bocchoris was put to death by Sabbacon, and his successors Psammetichus and Nechao, whose dates are well known, were the only dynasty that held up its head after the Ethiopian invasion. With the dynasty of Bubastus we are left more to our own conjectures; if we *assume* that Sesonch is the same as Shishak of the Old Testament, whose date is known, we shall find that it expired B.C. 840. Now the geographical position of the cities will not allow us to suppose that the

Ethiopians conquered Bubastus, for they had not yet conquered Thebes: nor, secondly, can we suppose that the successors of Rameses had extended their territory in this direction; for, on the other hand, we learn from Herodotus and Diodorus Siculus that they had lost Memphis, which was under the Saitic kings: and, thirdly, at a time when Manetho does not even consider that Memphis and Sais had made themselves independent, it is not probable that either of those cities had conquered Bubastus: hence, we have only the other case left, to suppose that the dynasty of Tanis, which even a century before had made itself independent of Thebes, had in the year B.C. 840, conquered Bubastus. The geographical position of the two cities makes this not improbable, particularly when we consider that the limits of kingdoms are generally fixed by physical and consequently unchangeable circumstances, and Pliny (lib. v.) tells us that when Egypt was divided into three parts, the first was the Thebais; the second Bubastus, Sethrium and Tanis; and the third Memphis and Sais.

It will be further seen that the dynasties of Tanis began about B.C. 910, which is only a few years earlier than the death of Rampsinitus, when, according to Herodotus, the quiet succession of Egyptian kings ceased; hence it would seem probable that, before this time, the Theban kings still ruled over Tanis, and indeed there are no other kings to whom we can assign that city, as it is improbable that the successors of Sesonchis, whose names were unknown to the historian, should have had any extended sway.

There were two dynasties of Shepherd kings; the fifteenth, which is the most important, as their names have been preserved, and the seventeenth, of which we have no names. Of these there were two expulsions, the first by Amosis, who made himself master of all Egypt, and the second by Amenophis, one hundred and fifty years later: hence we are led to conclude that the seventeenth dynasty consisted only of the despised few who were allowed to remain in Arabia [between the Red Sea and the Nile], and that it was the fifteenth dynasty which Amosis expelled. Manetho allows two hundred and eighty years to these six kings; but, as the number of kings is much more to be trusted to than the length of their reigns, I have, in the Chart of History, only allowed them one hundred and eighty years, which is thirty years instead of forty-seven years each; and this has the advantage of making their residence in Egypt take place between the reigns of the two great conquerors of Lower Egypt.

They are called Phenician, that is, of the same race as the inhabitants of Palestine before the conquest of that country by the Jews; a nomad race of herdsmen, who, instead of tilling the soil when their flocks had consumed the herbage, wandered about in search of fresh pasture, with no very settled notions of property; and who, in the eyes of nations who cultivated the ground, like the Egyptians, were only less hateful than the hunting tribes, such as we may suppose the Arabs and the Assyrians, the descendants of Nimrod, to have been at that time, against the latter of whom, Manetho tells us, the Shepherds themselves found it necessary to fortify their cities both in Egypt and after their expulsion.

Assigning this date to the Hycsos or Shepherd kings, their reign in Egypt falls, if we take the genealogy of David for our guide in the Hebrew chronology, about to the time of Abraham and Joseph; but there is considerable difficulty in reconciling this history with the Old Testament. They had possession of Memphis and Avaris, a city near Bubastus, and made Upper and Lower Egypt tributary; but had they possession of all Lower Egypt? had they the district where Joseph dwelt? I think not; I imagine that they only held a few fortified cities. They could not have been expelled before the time of Joseph, as the peaceable trading intercourse between the Egyptians and Arabs still existed (Genesis, xxxvii. 28): yet Joseph certainly dwelt among native Egyptians, to whom shepherds were an abomination (Genesis, xlvi. 34); and he thought that his brothers would be hurt in the opinion of the Egyptians if they were known to be shepherds.

Then it appears that the expulsion of the Shepherds took place between the death of Joseph and the birth of Moses, when a king came to the throne " who knew not Joseph," at the time that the kings of Thebes made themselves masters of the lower region.

Part of this race, the seventeenth dynasty, were allowed to remain in the district of Bubastus, till their final expulsion by Amenophis II., when these Arabs or *mixed people* went out with the Jews under Moses.

The sixteenth dynasty of Hellenic Shepherd kings, who were no doubt Greek colonists on the coast, held their settlements for just the same length of time that the Phenicians did; hence we naturally conclude that they were expelled at the same time. We are not told in what part of the Delta they dwelt, but it was probably in Sais, the part always most connected with Greece.

Nor are we told where they settled when expelled; and it is perhaps useless to conjecture respecting a migration which took place some centuries before the Trojan War: but, if we look round the coasts of the Mediterranean for Greek colonists with any peculiarities such as we might suppose a residence of some centuries in Egypt would have given them, we cannot but fix upon the Etrurians; a people who wrote from right to left, and omitted the short vowels; whose numerals, which we call Roman, were strictly hieroglyphic, there being one character for unit, one for ten, one for a hundred, and these were repeated as often as required, while other nations, and even the Egyptians in later days, as in the enchorial writing on the papyri, had a different character for each of the units; a people who had a year determined with astronomical precision without regard to lunar changes; who alone rivalled the Egyptians in their works for irrigation—witness the Po and Arno; who, like the Egyptians, have left us *scarabœi* cut in stone; who alone constructed arches between the time of the Theban and the Roman kings; whose kings were priests, and whose structures were cyclopean; and whose tombs, as of Porsenna and the Horatii, were pyramids.—See Niebuhr, Winkelman, &c.

On such speculations as these, however, no reliance can be placed in the absence of all tradition.

But to return to Manetho. With the earlier Theban dynasties, we are obliged to have recourse to conjecture; those of anonymous kings I reject as repetitions, and make the eleventh and twelfth immediately precede the seventeenth. To be exact, Sesostris the conqueror ought to precede the taking of Lower Egypt by the Phenicians, whereas by shortening the reigns of the Shepherd kings we still make Sesonkosis alone precede this invasion. But I would wish to alter the order of the first four kings to make them agree with the names in the Theban lists, which we shall hereafter see make the great conqueror the first in the twelfth dynasty, instead of the third. This disagreement is not great, as I consider the two names Sesostris and Sesonkosis the same, which we have already had occasion to remark.

The two Thinite dynasties together lasted five hundred and forty years; and, as we must suppose that This lost its independence when Thebes rose under Amosis, who could hardly have expelled the Shepherd kings from Memphis unless he were master of the intervening country, we must place Menes, the first king of This, at about B.C. 1960. The city of This was near to Abydus, if, indeed, it was not the same city; at any rate its importance was gone before Abydus rose, and it must have ceased to exist when Abydus was made the second capital of Egypt by Rameses II. It is never mentioned in connection with any later event: it continued, however, to give its name to the *nomos* or district, and in the time of Pliny Abydus was the capital of the Thinite nome.

The fifth dynasty reigned for two hundred and forty-eight years at Elephantine, a city so near the capital of Upper Egypt that we cannot hesitate to suppose that it fell on the first rise of Thebes under Amosis, and if so, this dynasty began about B.C. 1700, and lasted till his reign. This state, which might be called indifferently Philæ or Elephantine, was no doubt the state called by Isaiah (chap. lxvi. 19) Pul, which is mentioned in connection with Lud (Ethiopia); Pul being the same word as Philæ, and being the Hebrew, and no doubt the Ethiopic, for *elephant*.

The ninth and tenth dynasties are of Heracleopolis, and lasted either two hundred and eighty-five or five hundred and ninety-four years, a discordance so great that it is difficult to conjecture anything about them.

With exactly the same discordance, the fourteenth dynasty of Xois lasted one hundred and eighty-four or four hundred and eighty-four years; probably both of these fell under Amosis: and, if we grant them the longer periods, it is most probable that they did not consist of independent sovereigns, but merely of priests ruling over their respective cities.

The dynasties of Memphis are not easily explained; they ended with Queen Nitocris, who, if she is rightly identified with a queen whose name is found in the inscriptions, is of as great importance among the buildings of Thebes as in the pages of the historians. She made herself mistress of Thebes between the reign of Misaphris and that of Misphragmuthosis. Whether the three dynasties of Memphis followed one another without interruption is doubtful, because the Shepherd kings appear to have held Memphis till the reign of Amosis. Hence I have not ventured to insert these dynasties in the Chart of History.

To recapitulate: as our author has throughout given us his lists of kings as if the dynasties followed one another in continued succession through a period of several thousand years, and yet we find upon examination that, in some cases, they certainly were contemporaneous, we are left at liberty to arrange the whole in the best way we can, always in case of doubt leaning to that decision which places the events least backward in point of time. With this view of the case it would seem that Manetho's history begins about B.C. 1900, at which time there were several independent districts ruled over by their respective kings; that about B. C. 1600, Sesostris [or Sesonkosis] conquered all Egypt, marching into Asia; that soon afterwards the Phenicians or Arabs obtained possession of Memphis, and some other parts of Lower Egypt, making the rest of the country which they did not possess pay tribute. At this time Joseph lived in Egypt, as prime minister of one of the kings of Lower Egypt, who was independent of these Phenicians. About B. C. 1400, Amosis, king of Thebes, made himself master of both regions, expelling the Phenician herdsmen, and laid the foundation of the grandeur of Thebes and all Egypt, and of a race of kings who reigned for above four hundred years. One of these, Amenophis II., expelled the Jews and the few Phenicians who had been allowed to remain as slaves for one hundred and fifty years after the great expulsion.

About the year B.C. 980 Sesonchis of Bubastus made himself independent, and for the next two hundred years the country was divided into various independent states,—sometimes a king of Thebes, sometimes a king of Tanis, sometimes a king of Bubastus making himself master of the whole of Egypt.

It was probably in consequence of this civil discord that about B.C. 750 the Ethiopians were enabled to conquer Egypt. They held it about fifty years, and lost it, not by the rise of an Egyptian conqueror, but from their own weakness. After this, Thebes lost its importance; the sceptre passed to Lower Egypt, and the kings of Sais ruled over the Upper and Lower region, till the country was conquered by Cambyses. The Persians governed Egypt as a province for two hundred years, till Alexander the Great took it, with, however, the occasional interruption of a native prince making himself independent.

If we now turn back to Herodotus we shall find that, in his connected series of kings, no one before the invasion by the Ethiopians agrees in name with any one in Manetho; but this is not remarkable. Manetho obtained his information from Thebes, and Herodotus from Memphis; and the priests of Vulcan, whom Herodotus considered independent sovereigns at Memphis, were not recognized as such by Manetho. On comparing the two historians together we find (see the Chart of History) that Mœris agrees in point of time with Mephres or Misaphris, Sesostris with Sesonchis, Phero [Pharaoh] with Rameses III, and Rampsinitus with Thuoris, Rameses V.; and, when we come to the consideration of the inscriptions, we shall see additional reasons for believing that these kings are identical.

The independence of Memphis after the death of Rampsinitus, which is inferred from the account of Herodotus, is a very important circumstance; it proves that the descendants of Rameses had lost the whole of Lower Egypt, to which Memphis was the key; that Upper Egypt, which was then ruled over by kings whose names Manetho has not recorded, was splendid rather by the recollection of times then past than by its present power. Possibly the growing importance of navigation and of its maritime position might be one of the causes of the rise of Lower Egypt about this time; at any rate, with the independence of Memphis, the Delta, that granary of all Egypt and of the neighbouring countries, was lost to Thebes; the narrow valley of the Nile was probably far from able to support its large population, notwithstanding the great attention given to agriculture and irrigation. Thebes rose with the conquest of Memphis in the reign of Amosis, and fell with its loss at the death of Rampsinitus; and no doubt from that time found it difficult to defend itself against its Ethiopian neighbours.

The separation between Upper and Lower Egypt must have been important also in another point of view; it must have closed the navigation of the Nile, that great canal by which the wealth of India flowed towards Europe. The trade-winds would readily connect the mouth of the Indus and the Red Sea. The caravans crossed the desert to the Nile sometimes in Ethiopia to Meroe the capital of that country, and the merchandize then descended the river to the Mediterranean, enriching the cities on its banks; another passage across the desert was direct to Thebes, from the city on the Red Sea, which was afterwards called Berenice; and a third was from Cosseir to Coptos. The Oases, also, were resting-places for the caravans which crossed the desert on the west of Egypt, bringing merchandize to the Nile, to take advantage of the water carriage. With the civil war this stream of merchandize, one of the great causes of the wealth of Egypt, must have ceased; the trade of

India soon found other channels, of which one was up the Red Sea, through Arabia Nabatæa, by Petra, to Jerusalem and Tyre. The two causes operated at once; the loss of Lower Egypt and Ethiopia closed the navigation of the Nile, and the loss of Arabia opened the route by Petra.

Jerusalem and Tyre gained the trade which Thebes lost. Solomon built his mercantile navies on the Red Sea, which Hiram manned for him with his Tyrian sailors (1 Kings, ix. 27). They jointly imported gold, silver, ivory, apes, and peacocks, for which, the voyage out and home consumed three years (1 Kings, x. 22); and also spice from Arabia: the whole of this trade rose suddenly and fell as suddenly, for the successor of Solomon was not powerful enough to keep open the route by Petra to the Red Sea.

THE GENEALOGICAL TABLET OF KINGS AT ABYDUS.

THE splendid remains of the temples, palaces, tombs, and obelisks of Upper Egypt, at the same time that they prove the civilization and wealth of the country, teach us, by their numerous hieroglyphical inscriptions, the names of the sovereigns by whose enterprise and taste these stupendous buildings were raised; and in many cases add their parentage, their queens, and their predecessors on the throne.

The most valuable record of this kind is a tablet discovered at Abydus, by Mr. W. J. Bankes, which is a list of the kings of the Thebaid, arranged in the order of their succession (see Plate III.). It is broken in part, but seems to have contained, when perfect, seventy-eight ovals or names. It may be remarked, that the name of a king, when written at length, consists of three parts; first, a square name, which seems to have been the least essential of the three, and the most often omitted: secondly, an oval containing a name, which to us is only symbolic, or a picture, whatever it may have been to the Egyptians themselves; and this name is the one most often used in the historical inscriptions: and, thirdly, the phonetic name or oval, containing a number of letters which may be spelt and pronounced; and this is the only one which we can compare with the names handed down to us by the ancient authors, for, whenever the symbolic oval occurs alone, we can only so use it when we have already learnt the phonetic name belonging to it, by finding the two ovals together in some other inscription. The square name is usually preceded by an eagle and ball, the symbolic name by a twig and insect, and the phonetic name by a goose and ball. These three groups of characters must each be interpreted *king*, for want of knowing the distinction between them. Now it is to the learned industry of Mr. Wilkinson, who has collected the complete names of the kings, from the various monuments, that we are indebted for being able to determine the phonetic name belonging to each symbolic name.

But, to return to the Tablet of Abydus (Plate III.), it will be seen by the ornamental titles accompanying the ovals, that those in the second row purport to be the symbolic names, and those in the last row the symbolic and phonetic names in pairs. But our knowledge of the names of kings will further teach us that the last two ovals in the middle row are a pair, or complete name; and that it is only for pictorial reasons, or uniformity, that the sculptor has placed them like single names. Now, taking this view of it, and counting the blanks or absent ovals, as restored in the drawing, we shall find fifty single symbolic ovals, and fourteen pairs; each pair containing the symbolic oval, followed by the phonetic oval. The sitting figures under the names have on their heads the crowns of Upper and Lower Egypt, showing that the kings possessed or claimed that extent of territory.

The researches of Mr. Wilkinson and other travellers have supplied us, from the buildings of Thebes, with a continuation of the series from the end of the second line, which, however, appears to differ from the names on the unbroken part of the third line; and also with some of the missing names at the beginning of the second line.

In Plate IV. we have the names of the kings from No. 35 to No. 51 inclusive, from the Tablet of Abydus, numbered as in Plate III., preceded by three from the Tablet of Karnak, which are all with which we have Theban kings in Manetho early enough to compare, and followed by five more from the Theban inscriptions. Each of these names is a pair; the phonetic ovals may be spelt alphabetically, as will be explained when we come to the subject of Hieroglyphics, and may be compared with Manetho's dynasties as follows:

FROM MANETHO.	FROM THE SCULPTURES.
11th *Dynasty*.	Plate IV.
16. Amenemes [L]	A. Name not understood.
12th *Dynasty*.	
1. Geson Gosis, or Sesonkosis, son of Amenemes.	B. Osirtesen [L], king of Upper and Lower Egypt.
2. Amenemes [IL]	C. Amunmai-thor [L]
3. Sesostris, who conquered Asia.	35. Amunmai-thor [IL]
4. Lacharis.	36. Osirtesen [IL]
5. Ammeres.	37. Osirtesen [III.]

THE TABLET OF ABYDUS.

6. Amenemes [III.]
7. Scemiophris, his sister.
   Alisphragmuthosis.

38. Amunmai-thor [III.]
    Not in the Tablet.
    Not in the Tablet.

The agreement here is not so good as we could wish; the end of the name Amenem-thor is doubtful. Mr. Wilkinson reads it Amunmai-gori; Manetho seems to have avoided the difficulty, by dropping the last syllable and calling it Amenemes. Ses-ostris and Ses-onkosis are probably each Osirtesen. Sesostris is evidently the Sesoosis of Diodorus, who, like the god Osiris, conquered India beyond the Ganges, and whose name acquired a fabulous celebrity.

FROM MANETHO.
18th *Dynasty*.
1. Amosis, or Amos.
2. Chebros, his son.
3. Amenophis [L]
4. Amensis, his sister.
5. Misaphris, or Mephres.
   (Probably Nitocris of the 6th dynasty of Memphis.)
6. Misphragmuthosis.
7. Tuthmosis.
8. Amenophis [IL], of the
9. Horus.   [musical statue.
10. Acenchres, his daughter.
11. Rathos, his son.

12. Acencheres, or Chebres.
13. Acencheres, or Acherres.
14. Armeses, Miamous.

FROM THE SCULPTURES.
[found.
39. Phonetic oval not yet
40. Amos.
41. Amenothph [L]
    Not in the Tablet.
42. Thothmosis [I.]
    Queen Amun Neitgori, on the Theban buildings.
43. Thothmosis [IL]
44. Thothmosis [III.]
45. Amenothph [IL]
46. Thothmosis [IV.]
    Not in the Tablet.
47. Amenothph [III.], of the musical statue.
    Not in the Tablet.
    Not in the Tablet.
48. Amunmai Anamek.

15. Armeses, or Rameses [I.]
16. Amenophis.

19th *Dynasty.*

1. Sethos, or Rameses [II.]
2. Rapsases.
3. Ammenephthes.

Not mentioned by Manetho.
4. Rameses [III.]
5. Ammenemes.
6. Thuoris.

20th *Dynasty* of 7 or 12 *kings.*

1. Anonymous.
2.   ditto.
3.   ditto.
4.   ditto.
5.   ditto.
6.   ditto.
7.   ditto.
8.   ditto.

49. Rameses [L]
50. Amunmai Amunaan.
51. Amunmai Rameses [II. or the Great].
D. Ra-Amunoph?
E. Oeimenephthah, or Oseimenphthah.
F. Osirita Ramerer Amunmai?
G. Rameses [III.], his son.
H. Amunmai Rameses [IV.]
Rameses [V.]

Rameses [VI.]
   ditto? [VII.]
   ditto? [VIII.]
   ditto [IX.]
   ditto [X.]
Ameses?
Amunmai——?
Ameses?

The agreement of the names in the eighteenth dynasty is very striking, the order is the same in each: the four queens are all wanting in the Tablet; for, as Acenchres, No. 10, is a queen, probably No. 12 and No. 13 are so also. Chebros perhaps bore the name of his father; the names on the Tablet are obviously the ceremonial titles, which in all ages and countries have been more uniform and less distinctive (before the modern custom arose of adding numerals), while the historian, whose names are in the other column, of course dropped the names of Rameses, Thothmosis, and Amenothph, and used those by which individually the kings were best known. Hence I consider the only disagreement in the eighteenth dynasty is the mistake of Manetho in considering Amenoph II. as the king whose statue at Thebes has been in all ages so celebrated. The formation of the word Misphragmuthosis explains how he and his predecessor were named Tuthmosis. In the nineteenth dynasty the sameness of the hieroglyphical names makes the agreement or disagreement less obvious and less important.

The consideration of the twentieth dynasty confirms the view taken of it in page 53, that the greatness of the family of Rameses was past; had their actions been worth remembering, or sufficient to distinguish one from the other, the historian would have known their names, and on the Tablet they would scarcely have relied on their being the descendants, or perhaps only the successors, of Rameses the Great, as their best claim to the notice of posterity.

The hieroglyphical inscriptions very frequently tell us the relationship of one king to another, which is in some cases important; thus the three kings who succeeded Rameses III. were brothers (see Wilkinson's *Materia Hieroglyphica*, Part II.), which explains why their reigns were so short, as they were all of the same generation, for Manetho allows only one hundred and thirty-five or one hundred and seventy-two years to the seven or twelve kings of the twentieth dynasty. Again, Mr. Wilkinson finds from inscriptions on other monuments (see *Materia Hieroglyphica*), that Rathos (No. 47 of the Tablet of Abydus) was preceded by a queen and followed by a brother, who are not mentioned in the Tablet nor in the other lists of kings: now, on turning to Manetho's list, we find that Rathos was preceded by his sister Acenchres, and followed by another of that name, the two circumstances agreeing, with the exception, perhaps, of the sex of one of the individuals.

It is not difficult to frame reasons why kings' names are wanting in the chronological lists: they perhaps reigned for only a few months. It was probably the custom in these early times, as was known to be the case in Egypt at a later time, to call each civil year the first, second, or third of Rameses, as the case might be, without considering on what day he came to the throne, and so it frequently happened that a king who only reigned a few months did not give his name to the year, and then, though he is not forgotten by the historian, he is omitted by the chronologist. To illustrate this with a known instance, Ptolemy only enumerates eight Persian kings, from Cambyses to Darius Codomanus inclusive, stating how many whole years each reigned, or rather to how many years each king gave his name, as if each came to the throne on the first day of the civil year; and in this case it will be seen that three kings were omitted who reigned only a few months each. Or possibly the lists may be genealogical, which is certainly the case in some instances, and contain not all the king's predecessors but only his progenitors.

If we compare the English kings, from the death of Stephen to the present time, with the Theban kings in Manetho, from Amosis to the Ethiopian invasion, in each case about six hundred and eighty years, we find

In England:	In Thebes:
30	29 or 34 sovereigns.
4	4 queens.
4	2 pairs of brothers or sisters, succeeding one another.
1	1 set of three brothers or sisters.
4	3 dynasties.

William and Mary have been counted as a queen and a Stuart. The English dynasties are Plantagenet, Tudor, Stuart, and Guelph.

Thus we see that, if we take the mean number of years for the dynasties, and the mean number of kings in the last dynasty, the agreement in length of reigns with those of the English kings is very close,—twenty-two years and a half each reign.

THE EGYPTIAN BUILDINGS.

THERE remain to us two methods of estimating the power and wealth of the individual kings of Egypt: these are, first, the number and magnificence of the buildings erected by each, and the extent of territory in which their inscriptions are found, and, secondly, the particulars of these inscriptions. The former is much the more satisfactory, as the name of the builder of each monument is more certainly known from his inscriptions than the extent of his conquests. For, if we could more depend upon the reading of the inscriptions than we can, we still might be misled by the exaggerations of flattery.

Almost all the buildings, with the exception of the pyramids, contain the names of the kings who built them; and for this information I am principally indebted to Mr. Wilkinson's description of Thebes and Egypt.

As authors are not agreed on the mode in which some of the names are to be read, I shall in each case give the number by which the name is designated, in Plate IV. The number then will represent the hieroglyphical name, which is the same in all authors; the name of the king will differ according to the force which is attributed to the hieroglyphical characters in the phonetic oval, or according to which king in Manetho's list it is supposed to correspond with.

THE EGYPTIAN BUILDINGS.

The name of Osirtesen I. (B. Plate IV.) is found on the great temple of Karnak (Thebes)—he was probably the builder of the oldest part of it; on an obelisk near Biggig, a little to the north of Hermopolis; and again on an obelisk near Heliopolis below Memphis; his rule would therefore seem to have extended from Thebes to Heliopolis. This extent of dominion, and the near accordance in point of time, makes it probable that he is the Sesostris (Ses-Osirtis?) of Manetho, who conquered Asia. See p. 38. Some writers, however, have thought the name on the obelisk at Heliopolis to be Osorkon I., the son of Sesonchis; if so, it might be the obelisk mentioned by Herodotus, set up by the son of Sesostris in front of the temple of the Sun.

Amunmai-thor II. (35) and Osirtesen II. (36) are found upon a tablet near to Cosseir on the Red Sea, about the same latitude as Koptos; a circumstance of great importance, as showing the early time at which the Egyptians had settled on that coast, obviously for the purpose of trade, to carry the produce of India by the shortest route from the Red Sea to Thebes, and thence down their great navigable river to the Greek and Phenician merchants who frequented the cities of the Delta.

Amenothph I. (41) has a tomb amongst the other royal tombs near Thebes, ornamented with well-designed statues and sculptures in high relief. A funeral procession by water, in which a mummy lies in one of the boats, is represented on the walls, which is worthy of notice as a proof of the very early existence of that custom, from which the Greeks borrowed the idea of Charon's boat.

The royal tombs at Thebes are excavations in the hills of the neighbourhood, closed with such care that but few were entered by the Romans—some of them have been opened by modern travellers after having been closed three thousand years, and, notwithstanding this peculiarity in their construction, in the interior they have spacious rooms ornamented with columns, sculptures, and paintings; only four or five of them appear to have been finished.

Thothmosis I. (42) made some additions to the great temple at Karnak (Thebes), mentioned under Osirtesen I.: he also built at Tombos in Ethiopia.

I incline to the opinion that this king made the lake of Mœris available for purposes of irrigation by means of the canals, since I would identify him with Misaphris, or Mephres, of Manetho, and Mœris of Herodotus and Diodorus, who constructed the canals.

A queen named Nitocris, not mentioned in the Tablet of Abydus, appears to have followed Thothmosis I. She was named, according to Mr. Wilkinson, Amun-neitgori; but, according to Champollion, this was not a queen but a regent, named Amenenthe. That she was an usurper or conqueror of Thebes is proved by her successor Thothmosis II. having in some instances had her name erased, and his own substituted in its place. She was one of the more powerful sovereigns of Egypt, and a great builder: she erected two obelisks at Karnak, founded the temple of Dayr el Bahree, and founded or added to a small temple at Medinet Abu (all in Thebes). She is probably the Queen Nitocris of Manetho and Herodotus, the first syllable of whose name, according to Eratosthenes, was Neith, the name of the goddess, as it is also of the word Neitgori.

Thothmosis II. (43) appears to have added to the buildings, or at least to the sculptures of the temple at Medinet Abu; he also built a temple at Samneh in Ethiopia.

Thothmosis III. (44) also added to the palace at Medinet Abu, and built at Memphis, at Heliopolis, and at Samneh in Ethiopia; there is also a statue of him at Talmis in Ethiopia. His excavated tomb at Thebes is remarkable for the representation of a procession of men bearing tribute to the king, whose colour and costume are intended to distinguish the different tributary nations : 1st. Men with black and some with red complexions, in short dresses, bringing ivory, apes, leopards' skins, &c. (Asiatics?); 2d. Men of a light red colour, with long black curled hair, no beards; their dress a short apron and rich sandals; their gifts costly, of vases, necklaces, &c.; 3d. Others with gifts of rings, hides, apes, leopards, ivory, ostrich eggs and feathers, a camelopard, hounds with handsome collars, and long-horned oxen (Ethiopians); 4th. Men of a white nation with short beard and white dress, bringing the gifts of a civilized people from a cold climate, such as gloves, vases, a bear, an elephant, a chariot and horses; 5th. Egyptians.

At the town of Coptos there is a granite pillar bearing the name of this king; and at Thebes a brick arch (Hoskins's Travels), a circumstance of extreme interest when we remember that the Greeks appear to have been ignorant of its construction.

Amenothph II. (45); his tomb at Thebes is in the best style of Egyptian art, both as relates to the vases and borders, and also to the figures. His name is found upon a temple near to Apollinopolis Parva, upon another temple at Eilethyas (El Kab), and upon a third at Elephantine.

Thothmosis IV. (46) built the small temple between the fore legs of the colossal Sphinx near Memphis, and therefore is conjectured to have been the king who had the rock carved into the form of a sphinx, though it is more probable that the sphinx was formed long before the temple was built. His name is found at El Berkel the capital of Ethiopia. In an excavated temple at Silsilis he is represented as being carried in a palanquin accompanied by his fan-bearers, receiving the homage of various conquered nations.

THE EGYPTIAN BUILDINGS. 65

Amenothph III. (47) is the king whose colossal statue at Thebes is so celebrated for its uttering musical sounds. On the base of this statue is a variety of inscriptions, Latin, Greek, and hieroglyphical. Most of the Latin and Greek inscriptions record that the writers, who were European travellers, had heard the statue utter its famed musical sounds, and in these it is called the statue of Memnon, or Hamenoth, or Phamenoph. From the hieroglyphics we learn that it was a statue of Amenothph (No. 47 of Plate IV.); and Pausanias was informed that it was the statue of Phamenoph, and not of Memnon (Miamon Rameses). The initial PH in Phamenoph is the Coptic article, and the two consonants with which Amenothph ends explain the final letters of Hamenoth and Phamenoph. One inscription informs us that the statue was overthrown by Cambyses. It is of gritstone or breccia, and though sitting is about sixty feet high; and it may be remarked, for the sake of comparison, that the clenched fist of red granite in the British Museum belonged to a statue sixty-five feet high when standing (Flaxman's Lectures). There are several statues of this king in the British Museum, No. 21, a sitting figure; No. 16, the legs of a mutilated statue; Nos. 37, 57, and 88, sitting figures with tigers' heads. He was the founder of the palace at Karnak, which was afterwards enlarged, or rather rebuilt, by Rameses II., and he built more in Ethiopia than any other of the Egyptian kings.

This king appears to have been preceded by a queen regnant and succeeded by a brother, neither of whom are mentioned on the Tablet of Abydus: may not these be Nos. 10 and 12 of Manetho?

Amonmai Anamek (48). Sculpture by this king is found at Karnak; and there is in the British Museum a small statue of him,

K

a standing figure under the arm of the god Chem, called by the Greeks Pan; it is No. 5 in the collection.

Rameses I. (49); his tomb is amongst those of the other kings at Thebes.

Amonmai Amonaan (50), called by Champollion and Mr. Wilkinson Osiri I. from another phonetic oval, a synonym of this name. The sculptures and buildings of this king are remarkably beautiful; his tomb is perhaps the handsomest at Thebes, and well known under the name of Belzoni's, being first opened by that traveller: it contained the alabaster coffin, miscalled sarcophagus, now in Sir John Soane's Museum. (The Egyptians, who embalmed the body with such care, would be the last people to use a sarcophagus, and indeed alabaster would not have the effect of destroying the body.) Among the paintings is a procession of red men, or Egyptians; white men with blue eyes, long bushy beards—a northern nation; black men—from the south; and again white men with blue eyes, pointed beards, and feathers in their hair—from the east. This king's additions to the great palace at Karnak are in the best style of Egyptian art; the sculptures represent at great length his wars and victories, probably over an eastern nation. He also began the palace at Abydus commonly called the Memnonium, and may be conjectured to be the king who first made Abydus share with Thebes the honour of being the capital of Upper Egypt.

Rameses II. or the Great (51) carried on his wars at least as successfully, and ornamented his capitals with as good taste, as his father who preceded him. Indeed this reign was the Augustan age of Egyptian art; it had arrived at its greatest beauty, and was not yet overloaded with ornament. He added to the temple at Luxor, and set up the obelisks in front of it. His palace at Thebes, called the Memnonium, yields to no building in Egypt for magnificence or architectural merit: it is the ruin which has the best claim to be considered the palace of Osymandyas, described in Diodorus. Champollion was of opinion that the number and ornaments of the rooms agreed as nearly as could be expected with the description in that author; and this opinion is strongly confirmed by the remark of Strabo, that some considered the Memnon of the Greeks and the Ismandes of the Egyptians as the same person, and by Rameses being succeeded by his seventh son, according to Mr. Wilkinson's Hieroglyphical Researches, while Diodorus tells us that Osymandyas was succeeded by his eighth—an agreement so close in a circumstance so peculiar as alone to be of great weight.

The temple of Osiris and palace called the Memnonium, both at Abydus, begun by his father, were for the most part built in this reign. His statues, mostly colossal, are very numerous in Upper Egypt, and one is at Memphis; several obelisks at Tanis bear his name. His tomb at Thebes is nearly filled with earth; but the sculptures on the Memnonium at Thebes, and on the palace at Karnak, are the great witnesses to the splendour of this reign. The king appears to be carrying on the wars of his father against the same Asiatic nations, with equal success. In one place " there is a corps of infantry in close array, flanked by a strong body of cha_ riots; and a camp, indicated by a rampart of Egyptian shields, with a wicker gateway guarded by four companies of sentries, who are on duty on the inner side, forms the most interesting object of this picture: here the booty taken from the enemy is collected; oxen, chariots, plaustra, horses, asses, sacks of gold, representing the confusion after a battle, and the richness of the spoil is expressed by the weight of a bag of money under which an ass is about to fall. One chief is receiving the salutation of a foot soldier; another, seated amidst the spoil, strings his bow; and a sutler suspends a water-skin on a pole he has fixed in the ground. Below this a body of infantry marches homewards; and beyond them the king, attended by his fan-bearers (see Hieroglyphical Collections of Egyptain Society), holds forth his hand to receive the homage of the priest and principal persons, who approach his throne to congratulate his return."

In another picture there is a " battle, in which the use of the ladder and of the testudo throw considerable light on the mode of warfare at this early period. The town, situated on a lofty rock, is obstinately defended, and many are hurled headlong from its walls by the spears, arrows, and stones of the besieged; they, however, on the nearer approach of the Egyptian king, are obliged to sue for peace, and send heralds."—Wilkinson.

The enemy are a lighter coloured race than the Egyptians, and in dress and features are the same as the prisoners of Tirhakah, whom we know to be Assyrians. When the cities are taken by assault the king fights on foot with spear and shield, otherwise in a chariot.

That this king ruled over Ethiopia is fully proved by his numerous buildings and inscriptions in that country, but he can have no claim to the merit of having conquered it: he has repeatedly recorded his victories on his buildings there, in the same graphic manner that he has done at Thebes. At Isamboul he and three of his sons are seen each in a chariot with the horses at full gallop, in pursuit of the enemy, and afterwards they appear in triumph with negroes among their other prisoners. His obelisks are remarkably handsome, and as Pliny tells us that Suthis made four large obelisks at Thebes, we may consider them a confirmation of his being the Sethos of Manetho. In the British Museum the colossal head No. 19, a broken kneeling figure, No. 27, and a squatting figure, No. 46, are of this king. In all probability this is the king mentioned by

Tacitus under the name of Rhamses, and the sculptures described above those which were admired by Germanicus, and explained to him by the priests.

The words Memnonium, the name of his palace, and Memnon, a name by mistake applied to Amenothph in the case of the musical statue, are derived from Amonmai or Miamon, his prenomen; and he seems to be the original of the fabulous hero, the conqueror of Asia, known amongst the Greeks by the name of Memnon. Amenothph does not appear to have been a conqueror, or to have been known out of Egypt. The citadel of Susa in Persia was called the Memnonium, more probably from the celebrity which that name had acquired than from Rameses having really extended his conquests to that city.

Thus far we have proceeded, with but little difficulty, through a series of kings, confirmed by a variety of testimonies; 1st, by the Tablet of Abydus, made thirteen generations later than the king last mentioned; 2d, by the inscriptions at Medinet Abu, made four generations after him, by a king who claimed to have descended through this series; and 3d, by the inscription on the Memnonium at Thebes, where Rameses II. claims these as his ancestors: but here, unfortunately, the Tablet of Abydus is broken; one king's name is wholly gone and one partially, and we have only the Theban list to depend upon; and after the interval of these two reigns we find that the Tablet of Abydus no longer agrees with the Theban list, or with the names on the Theban buildings, and we are led to conjecture that Thebes and Abydus were no longer under the same king. Rameses II. had a palace called Memnonium, as we have seen, at each city; his third successor Rameses III. possibly reigned at Thebes only, though from his ruling over Memphis this may be doubted.

The names of the last three kings on the Tablet of Abydus have been partially erased with care, with the evident intention of supplying their places with some other names, a common Egyptian practice in the case of disputed claims to the throne: these are the eleventh, twelfth, and thirteenth from Rameses II. If the names to have been supplied were those of the Ethiopian kings, these kings of Abydus must have reigned longer than Manetho's twentieth dynasty of Thebes; if, as is most probable, of the Theban kings, it would prove a civil war. Nos. 62 and 64 are only partially erased, probably with the intention of inserting the names of some of the same family. The same has been done at Thebes, where the name of Amunmai —— ? the thirteenth from Rameses the Great, has been half erased.

But to return to the series of Theban kings.

(D.), who seems to have been the seventh son of Rameses the Great, succeeded his father at Thebes, at any rate, if not at Abydus. His name is doubtful, Pthah Amenoph or Ra-amenoph: his tomb at Thebes is in very good style of sculpture, and he contributed to the buildings at Eilethyas and Silsilis. The names of this king and of Osirita Remerer (F. of Plate IV.) occur upon a fluted column, No. 64 in the British Museum. No. 61 in the Museum is also a standing figure of this king.

Pthah Amun-pthah, the next king, is not in any of the lists; no doubt because, though a predecessor, he was not a progenitor of Rameses III., the list perhaps being genealogical: his tomb is at Thebes.

Osiramun-pthah (E.); his tomb at Thebes is in very good style; he added to the palace at Karnak. No. 26 in the British Museum is a youthful statue of this king, sitting, and without a beard, beautifully executed. I should rather read this name Oseimen-pthah, or Oeimen-pthah, and would conjecture that it was the name called by Diodorus, Osymandyas, and by Strabo, Ismandes : his tomb was one of those which had been entered at the time of Diodorus, but no building of his remains, which he supposed to be the celebrated palace of Osymandyas.

Osirita Remerer Amonmai (F.) follows in the genealogical lists, being the father of Rameses III., but he does not appear in Manetho's list of kings; his name is upon a fluted column, No. 64 of the British Museum, as mentioned above.

Rameses III. (H.) was, like his predecessor Rameses II., both a successful warrior and an enterprizing builder: his tomb is at Thebes; he added to the temple at Karnak, but his principal work was building the palace at Medinet Abu, one of the principal buildings in Thebes. It is ornamented by sculptures of an extremely curious historical character. In one place the king is surrounded by his harem; in another he is defeating his enemies: but the subject of greatest interest is the grand procession of the king to be crowned with the crown of Upper and Lower Egypt. He is borne on a canopy, and accompanied by the princes, the officers with fans, the priests, the scribes, and a military guard; the sceptres and insignia are borne before him, and incense is burnt behind him; then the king, wearing his helmet, sacrifices to Khem or Pan; the statue of the god is then carried, attended by twenty-two priests; the king follows on foot, and before the god is the sacred bull Apis, wearing the crown of the " Lower Country;" the queen is a spectator of the procession. The hieroglyphics describe the king as having put on the crown of the Upper and Lower regions, which he then wears for the first time.

When we recollect that this is a king of Upper Egypt, recording with great display his coronation with the double crown, and that the crown of Lower Egypt is particularly introduced on the sacred bull, we are almost led to believe that the event intended to be recorded is the recovery of Lower Egypt under the dominion of Thebes. This king I consider the Phero (Pharaoh) who, according to Herodotus, succeeded Sesostris at Memphis.

This was the florid time of Egyptian art, which rose and fell by the same steps that the ornamental arts of Greece and Rome have since done; being at first more rude and severe, attaining its greatest correctness under Rameses II., under Rameses III. becoming florid, and from that time declining, through neglect of correctness.

Seven successive kings of the name of Rameses followed Rameses III., and most of them have left their names on the Theban palaces of their ancestors. Whether they are the same kings as those of the name of Rameses on the Tablet of Abydus, and as the anonymous kings of Manetho's twentieth dynasty, we cannot tell; but the three authorities agree in the fact that they were not worthy of note. From the Tablet differing throughout from the names at Thebes, it is more probable that different branches of the same family claimed dominion at the two cities. I have not found any notice of their names being in sculpture on the buildings of Lower Egypt.

Sesonk or Shishank, for his name in the inscriptions has only the four consonants, has left his name upon several monuments at Thebes, more particularly the account of the captives taken by him in his wars in Syria (comp. 2 Chronicles, xii.), which are on the great temple at Karnak, near the account of the victories of Rameses II., and probably in imitation of that monarch. The name of one of these captives, represented, of course figuratively, with his arms tied behind him, is in hieroglyphics Judah Melek, or king of Judah, מלך יהדה. There is a sitting figure of this king in black basalt in the British Museum, No. 63, having a tiger's head; it is so like to those of Amenothph III., Nos. 37, 57, and 88, that it seems natural to suspect that he placed his name upon a statue of his predecessor, a practice not uncommon in Egypt. His tomb is unknown.

As this is the earliest king in Manetho's list whose date is known through the Old Testament, it becomes important to determine, by means of the inscriptions, what place he held in the series of Egyptian kings, not for the sake of determining the time when he lived, for that is one of our known points in the chronology, but for dating the other kings by means of him. He is not mentioned in any of the Theban lists; of course because he was not of the legitimate family. The names by which we find him called are

    Shishak - - - - - - - in the Old Testament;
    Shishank or Sesonk - - - in the inscriptions;
    Sesonchis - - - - - - in Manetho;
    Sesostris - - - - - - in Herodotus.

The first three are identical, with the exception of the N being omitted in the Old Testament; the last we have not now to do with; it is shown to be the same with the first, by their agreeing in date and actions. We have seen, in the Chart of History, that with the date which we have given to Thuoris, Shishak lived between the reigns of Rameses II. and Rameses III.; unfortunately the inscriptions have not yet been found to contain any exact information on this head, but it is something to find that they do not contradict it, and in some points go to confirm it. 1st. His name is found on the older buildings at Karnak, but not on the newer buildings at Medinet Abu, erected by Rameses III. 2d. Of the father of Rameses III. nothing else is known but that he is included in his son's genealogical lists; he is not mentioned by Manetho, who, to fill up the gap, makes Rameses III. reign for sixty years, while Mr. Wilkinson finds no inscription dated later than the forty-fourth of his reign: it is in this interval that I imagine Sesonchis reigned at Thebes. 3d. Rameses III. makes an express boast in his sculptures of having regained the crown of Lower Egypt. 4th. And, as the victorious Rameses III. is preceded by an almost anonymous father, so Sesonchis is succeeded by three anonymous kings; in each case the historian has left a gap to be filled up by our conjectures. All this, however, is no proof; it only serves to explain that there is no contradiction in placing Sesonchis, the conqueror of Thebes and Jerusalem, at a point of time when the Theban lists give us an unbroken series of kings of the family of Rameses. We have before seen that in the same manner all the Theban lists omit Queen Nitocris, a sovereign of nearly equal celebrity, for the same reason, because they were both usurpers.

From the time of Rameses III. till the invasion by the Ethiopians there is much obscurity, yet at the same time but little difficulty; we know of no one of the family of Rameses sufficiently powerful to be *de facto*, though every one of them claimed to be *de jure* king of Upper and Lower Egypt; we do not find their names in Lower Egypt, hence we are not surprised to find the successors of Sesonchis in possession of Bubastus, and occasionally, as we learn from the inscriptions, masters of Thebes.

Osorkon I., Takelothe, Osorkon II., Sesonk II., succeeded, and have left their names upon the buildings at Thebes, and are the only successors of Sesonk I. whose hieroglyphical names have been identified with those of the historians. There is a statue of Osorkon I. in the British Museum, No. 8. These four reigns cannot fill up the time from Sesonk, B.C. 940, to Sabbacon, B.C. 740;

hence I conclude that their reigns at Thebes were only intervals when the regular succession of the family of Rameses was broken. Rameses VI. and Rameses VII., the contemporaries of Takelothe, seem to be unknown on the buildings; so we are not surprised to find from the inscriptions that Takelothe reigned at Thebes, nor that a new dynasty had arisen at Tanis, of whom Osorkon II. and Sesonk II. (Osorchor and Psinaches of Manetho) were sufficiently powerful to hold Thebes; that Memphis, Sais, and Ethiopia were independent; and that there was a Cushite sovereign in the north of Arabia.

Sabbacon has left inscriptions at Thebes and at Abydus; and a Greek inscription at Aboo Simbel, by the Ionian and Carian auxiliaries of Psammetichus, proves that this king attempted to recover possession of that country.

To recapitulate, we learn from the monuments now remaining in Egypt, that the sovereigns of Upper Egypt at a very early time ornamented their capitals with costly and tasteful buildings, of a form peculiarly massive and durable; that they had possessions on the coast of the Red Sea, probably for purposes of commerce with the east; that in the reign of Amosis their rule extended over the Delta and the whole of what we now call Egypt; that as early as Thothmosis I. they held Ethiopia, which, if we may judge by the number of their buildings, was at first even more closely connected with them than Lower Egypt was; that from this time till the reign of Rameses III. the power and wealth of the country was very great, and almost all the splendid buildings of Upper Egypt which are older than the time of the Ptolemies were erected; that in the reign of Rameses II. their foreign conquests were very considerable, but that shortly after his reign the strength and extent of the kingdom began to lessen, although its magnificence lasted a century longer.

Ethiopia and Lower Egypt were lost about the same time, and when we next find all Egypt under one monarch, the seat of government was removed to the lower region, and the wealth and power of the country, which we learn from the historians was again very considerable, no longer displayed itself in architecture or sculpture.

Thus, in the early parts of the history the sculptures have been an important help; but as soon as Manetho, Herodotus, and Diodorus agree they need no such confirmation, while at the same time the decline of art and literature in Egypt make the information of the sculptures more scanty. The later kings continued adding their inscriptions to the buildings erected by the magnificence of their predecessors, and if they did not build or add to the monuments of their country they at least preserved them; even the Ethiopians were eager to place their names upon the monuments, and showed their respect to the arts of the conquered by their endeavour to imitate them, but on the Persian conquest of the country, the destruction of the buildings and statues appears to have been wanton and determined: we are as much surprised at the force which must have been used to dash to pieces the enormous colossal statues of granite, as we are at the patience which must have been required to make them.

The information gained from this examination of the buildings I have added to the Chart of History, Plate I., leaving the space of one reign before Rameses III., which is coloured as if ruled over by Sesonchis, and the rule of Rameses III. has been made to extend over Memphis, Tanis, and Sais. Ethiopia has been put under the rule of Thebes from Misaphris (Thothmosis I.) to Sethos (Rameses II.), and again during the reign of Psammetichus; but, as the exact time neither of the conquest nor loss of Ethiopia is known, the line is made to slope in each case to the time when it was certainly independent. After the Ethiopian dynasty, the countries have been coloured as if each were independent, as we know of no king before Psammetichus who was powerful enough to rule over all Egypt.

It will naturally be asked, by those who prefer the earlier dates for the Trojan War and birth of Moses, Why may we not leave the dynasties of Tanis and Bubastus as they stand in the Chart, and set back the Theban dynasties and Shepherds two centuries, making the family of Rameses end with the accession of Sesonchis; and Sesonchis and his successors rule over Thebes till the Ethiopian invasion, and place the kings of Diodorus in the room of those of Herodotus?

The answer is, 1st. That if the evidence in favour of the earlier and later dates of these events were *equal*, which, however, I would by no means grant, we should yet take the later. 2d. That it is improbable that the twentieth dynasty of Manetho, of whom the historian did not know the names, and of whom we can learn nothing from the monuments, should have ruled over Upper and Lower Egypt, while it may be argued that they did not even hold Abydus. 3d. That neither the historian nor the monuments can produce Theban successors of Sesonchis, sufficient to fill up the time from his death to the Ethiopian invasion, two events whose dates are well known. 4th. That the testimony of Herodotus is express, that Rampsinitus, who was no doubt a Rameses, was ruling quietly and prosperously over great part of Egypt, B.C. 900, which is fifty years after the time of Sesonk. It must, however, be acknowledged that one of the great desiderata in Egyptian chronology is an inscription or sculpture which shall determine the relative dates of Sesonk and the family of Rameses, since Sesonk or Shishak is the only king before the Ethiopian invasion whose name is certainly known upon the Theban monuments, and whose date is known with equal certainty from contemporary history.

The theory that Sesostris was Rameses II. cannot be held without entirely disregarding the chronology of Herodotus, and the same may be said of Sesoosis of Diodorus; the three kings agree in nothing except in being conquerors in the east. The monuments mention three great conquerors, Osirtesen I., Rameses II, and Sesonk; Manetho also mentions them under the names of Sesostris or Sesonkosis, Sethos or Rameses II, and Sesonchis; and Greek tradition mentions Osiris, or Bacchus, or Sesoosis (each of whom conquered India beyond the Ganges), Memnon, and Sesostris. Sesonchis conquered Palestine in the reign of Rehoboam; Rameses II. could hardly have conquered that country, because he is not mentioned in the Old Testament; Osirtesen I. lived before the Jewish nation was founded: thus the existence of the three separate kings is well established, and their actions, but more particularly the chronology, inform us that Sesoosis of Diodorus, who is evidently a fabulous hero, is probably Osirtesen L; that Memnon is Rameses the Great; and that Sesostris of Herodotus is Sesonk; however much the three heroes may be in some respects confounded.

THE PYRAMIDS.

No hieroglyphics are now met with upon the pyramids, to assist us in judging when they were built. Herodotus says that the three large pyramids near Memphis were built soon after the Trojan War; but adds, that they were not called by the names of the kings whom he says were the builders. Diodorus Siculus assigns nearly the same date to them, but adds that some authors differed about it. Manetho, however, whose opinion is in every thing entitled to great weight, says that they were built before the rise of the Theban empire, that is, many centuries earlier than Herodotus places them. Each historian considers them the work of kings who made Memphis their capital.

The sides of the pyramids exactly face the north, south, east, and west. The largest is four hundred and seventy-four feet high, and seven hundred and thirty-two feet is the measure of each side of the base. The stones of which it is built are large, and cemented.

The second pyramid is not so well built, though of the same materials; its height is four hundred and sixty-six feet, and base six hundred and ninety feet.

The third and smaller pyramid is built in steps, to which a casing of granite has been added.

The Sphinx stands nearly opposite to the second pyramid; besides which there are seven smaller pyramids.

In the neighbourhood are several tombs of kings and private persons, many of them with sculpture, hieroglyphics, and names of kings, all having a claim to be counted among the oldest sculptured buildings in Egypt.

Now the date of the pyramids in some measure rests on the question whether the different style of art, the absence of all hieroglyphics, and the circumstance of the tombs having their position regulated by the direction of the base of the pyramid, prove the pyramids to be the older monuments of the two. The tombs are judged from their style to be, some of the time of the splendour of Thebes, and some older.

Again, the Sphinx, which from its size we are led to class with the pyramids, was in all probability formed before the rise of Theban art at Memphis; for the temple by Thothmosis IV., which stands between the fore feet of the Sphinx, can hardly have been made at the same time with the stupendous monument to which it is but a paltry accompaniment. The tombs have the same relation to the pyramids which the temple has to the Sphinx.

In the Valley of Tombs near Thebes there are also brick pyramids, and there are many small brick pyramids in Ethiopia which were the tombs of the kings; these last are upon an average fifty feet square and fifty feet high, not placed with any regularity as regards the meridian; they are ornamented with sculptures and hieroglyphics similar to those of Upper Egypt, and Mr. Hoskins, who is in every respect well qualified to decide, pronounces them to be of an earlier style of art than any of the sculptures of Thebes.

From these considerations it seems probable that the pyramids near Memphis were built before the rise of the Theban splendour, that is, before the expulsion of the Shepherds. As it seems probable that the Shepherds only held armed possession of the country, they could hardly have been the builders of such stupendous works, which could not have been erected during the interruptions of war; and for the same reasons the pyramids could not have been erected by the native Egyptians while the Shepherds made the neighbouring cities tributary: hence we come to a conclusion which entirely agrees with Manetho's account, who says that they were built about twelve reigns before Queen Nitocris, or about B.C. 1700, by native kings who ruled at Memphis, several reigns before the Shepherds conquered the lower region.

The curious remark of Herodotus that they were called by the name of the shepherd Philitis, is not of sufficient weight against the foregoing reasons, to lead us to the conclusion that they were built by the above-mentioned Philistine Shepherds.

ERATOSTHENES.

SYNCELLUS has preserved some fragments of the History of Thebes by Eratosthenes, who lived two hundred years before Christ, about sixty years after Manetho: these consist of kings' names with their dates, of which very few agree with the names in other authors; but, as they purport to be translated into Greek from the names in the hieroglyphical inscriptions at Thebes, they deserve every attention. Some allowance may be made for the imperfect state in which we have these fragments.

Year of the World.   KINGS OF THEBES.

2900. 1. Mines of This, which is translated Eternal: he reigned 62 years.

2962. 2. Athothis, his son; which is translated (Ermogenes) Born of Mercury: he reigned 59 years.

3021. 3. Athothis: he reigned 32 years.

3053. 4. Dabies, the son of Athosis [Athothis]; which is translated Psilesteros: he reigned 19 years.

3072. 5. Pemphos, the son of Athothis; which is, Son of Hercules: he reigned 18 years.

3090. 6. Amachos Momcheiri, of Memphis; which is translated Full of excellence: he reigned 79 years.

3169. 7. Stoichos, his son; which is, Mars the fool: he reigned 6 years.

3175. 8. Gosormies; which is, Etesipantos: he reigned 30 yrs.

3205. 9. Mares, his son; which is, (Heliodorus) Gift of the Sun: he reigned 26 years.

3231. 10. Anoÿphes; which is, A common son: he reigned 20 years.

M

ERATOSTHENES.

3251. 11. Sirios; which is, Son of a maiden: he reigned 18 yrs.
3269. 12. Xnoubos Gneuros; which is, (Chryses the son of Chryses) Gold the son of gold: he reigned 22 yrs.
3291. 13. Rauosis; which is, Seizer of power: he reigned 13 years.
3304. 14. Biüris: he reigned 10 years.
3314. 15. Saophis Komatistes; according to some, Chrematistes: he reigned 29 years.
3343. 16. Sensaophis II.: he reigned 27 years.
3370. 17. Moscheris; Gift of the Sun: he reigned 31 years.
3401. 18. Mousthis: he reigned 33 years.
3434. 19. Pammos Archondes: he reigned 35 years.
3469. 20. Apappous, The great: he reigned 100 years to an hour.
3569. 21. Acheskos Okaras: reigned 1 year.
3570. 22. Nitocris, a queen; which is, Minerva the bearer of victory: she reigned 6 years.
3576. 23. Myrtœus Ammonodotos: reigned 22 years.
3598. 24. Thusimares, The powerful; which is, The Sun: he reigned 12 years.
3610. 25. Thinillos; which is, Enlarger of his father's power: he reigned 8 years.
3618. 26. Semphroucrates; which is, Hercules Harpocrates: he reigned 18 years.
3636. 27. Chouther Taurus; which is, King: reigned 7 years.
3643. 28. Meures: reigned 12 years.
3655. 29. Chomaephtha; which is, The world beloved by Vulcan: reigned 11 years.
3666. 30. Agkounios Ochuturannos: reigned 60 years.
3726. 31. Penteathuris; which is, Priest of Venus: reigned 42 years.

3768.	32.	Stamenemes II.: reigned 23 years.
3791.	33.	Sistosichermes. The power of Hercules: reigned 55 years.
3846.	34.	Maris: reigned 43 years.
3889.	35.	Siphoas, or Mercury the son of Vulcan: reigned 5 years.
3894.	36.	———— reigned 14 years.
3908.	37.	Phrouron, or Neilos: reigned 5 years.
3913.	38.	Amouthantaios: reigned 63 years.

In the case of several of these names, we have no difficulty in determining from what they are translated; thus, Helio-dorus may be Ra-meses; Ammono-dotus, Amen-othph; Taurus, Horus, spelt Thorus in the enchorial language; Maris, Mephres (Thothmosis I.); Mercury, Thothmosis II.; Stamenemes, Amonmai; Thusimares the Sun, Thuoris (Rameses V.)

This series of kings would be of great use in our chronological enquiries, if we could identify the names with those of Manetho; we could then determine what Eratosthenes meant by the " year of the world," and make use of his methodical arrangement of referring them all to a common epoch. But they seem to follow in a very different order from those of Manetho, and, if so, a complete agreement is impossible. I venture, however, to offer the following series, as agreeing pretty well with those of our other authorities, both in the names and the intervals at which they succeed one another.

Eratosthenes.	Chart of History, Plate I.
A.M.	B.C.
2900. Mines of This.	1960. Menes of This. See p. 50.
3269. Xnoubos Gneuros.	1610. Geson Gosis.

A.M.	B.C.
3469. Apappous.	1420. Apophis, the Shepherd king, who probably ruled over Thebes.
3570. Nitocris.	1320. Nitocris, the successor of Misaphris.
3636. Chouther Taurus.	1240. Horus, or Thorus.
3768. Stamenemes.	1090. Amonmai Amonaan.
3791. Sistosichermes.	1060. Sethos.
3913. The last king of the series.	900. The last Theban king mentioned by name.

A.M. 4860, - about B.C. 0 of our era.

If these, however, be considered as agreeing, the disagreement in other places is very important; though it is rather a confirmation of our chronology to find Thusimares, who is probably Thuoris the contemporary of the Trojan War, placed B.C. 1260, because that is about the time that Eratosthenes considered this war to have taken place, as we know from his fragments of Greek History.

FLAVIUS JOSEPHUS.

Lib. viii. cap. 2. MENEAS, the founder of Memphis, lived long before the time of our father Abraham, above one thousand three hundred years before Solomon.

The Hebrew jurisdiction formerly extended to Elan, a city near to Berenice, which is on the bay of the Red Sea called Ezon Geber.

Cap. 4. [Speaking of Sesostris and Shishak] Herodotus has mistaken the name of the king of Egypt who conquered Palestine-Syria.

Lib. x. cap. 2. Sennacherib, when laying siege to Pelusium, had raised his platforms almost to a level with the top of the walls, and was nearly ready for the assault, but withdrew his army, and retired to his own dominions, on hearing that Tirhakah, king of Ethiopia, was marching to the assistance of the Egyptians.

ARISTOTLE.

SESOSTRIS was the first king of Egypt who attempted to make a navigable canal from the Red Sea to the Nile; but he found that the sea was at a higher level than the river, for which reason he, and afterwards Darius, gave up the attempt.—*Meteor.* lib. i. c. 14.

Sesostris was the author of the distinction which was made in Egypt between the military and agricultural classes: he lived much before the time of Minos.—*De Repub.* lib. vii. cap. 10.

This attempt to connect the head of the Red Sea with the Mediterranean, by means of a canal cut through part of the Delta, arose probably from a wish on the part of a king of Lower Egypt to be able to bring the Indian trade through his dominions, at a time when the navigation of the Nile was interrupted by civil war or by the division of the country into separate kingdoms. No king of Upper Egypt would have planned any thing so injurious to the prosperity of his capital; but Sesostris might have wished to gain part of the trade which, if we are right in the date assigned to him, was now being enjoyed by Solomon, and Hiram king of Tyre. Darius also might have had a similar motive, finding his dominion over Upper Egypt not peaceable enough to keep open the navigation of the Nile; for no merchant in those days, or even centuries later, would have lengthened the difficult voyage on the Red Sea to use this canal, while the less hazardous navigation of the Nile was uninterrupted.

With respect to the two privileged orders, we have seen that the priests were a distinct class as early as the time of Joseph; consequently Aristotle is more likely to be right in saying that Sesostris separated the military from the rest of the nation, than Herodotus, who says that they both owed their privileges to this king. By the mention of Minos we learn the opinion of Aristotle, that Sesostris preceded the Trojan war by above sixty years.

DICÆARCHUS.

THE Greek scholiast to the fourth book of Apollonius Rhodius quotes Dicæarchus as saying, in his first book, that Sesonchosis lived two thousand five hundred years before Nileus, and Nileus four hundred and thirty-six years before the first Olympiad; and that he (Sesonchosis) made a law that no man should leave the occupation or trade of his father.

In his second book he says that Sesonchosis imitated the Greek customs, and made a law that no man should leave the occupation of his father.

The scholiast adds, that Sesonchosis was the same king as Sesostris mentioned in Herodotus.

STRABO.

SESOSTRIS conquered all Ethiopia to the cinnamon country, and his monuments, columns, and inscriptions yet remain.

Ismandes built the palace at Memphis called the Labyrinth.

Memnon built the palaces at Thebes and Abydus, the capitals of the Thebaid; each of these palaces was called the Memnonium; some, however, consider Memnon the same person as Ismandes. At Thebes are two colossal statues of this king, one of them thrown down; and Strabo, in company with Ælius Gallus and a multitude of friends and soldiers, heard the statue which was yet standing utter its famed musical sounds, about the first hour of the day.

Thon ruled in the Saitic nome when Menelaus arrived there.

Psammetichus was buried in the temple of Minerva at Sais.

Cambyses is repeatedly mentioned as the great destroyer and wanton mutilator of the buildings and monuments of all Egypt.

After Alexander succeeded Ptolemy the son of Lagus; then Philadelphus, Euergetes, Philopator, Epiphanes, and Philometor, the son always succeeding the father; then came Euergetes II., called Phiscon, the brother of Philometer; next Lathurus, and Auletes the father of Cleopatra: after Cleopatra Egypt was made a Roman province.

Egypt extended from the mouths of the Nile to the lesser cataract above Syene. The Thebaid is divided into ten nomes, middle Egypt into sixteen nomes, the Delta into ten nomes. The whole of the Delta is flooded for forty days by the Nile, and the houses built either on natural or artificial mounds: when it rises fourteen cubits it produces the greatest fertility, when only eight cubits it is followed by a scarcity. There was a Nilometer at Elephantine, a well built of solid masonry, μονολιθον, by the side of the Nile, in which the rise and fall of the water was noted by the scale which was engraved on the wall.

Egypt was originally the narrow strip of country below the lesser cataract, watered by the Nile; the country on the west was called

Libya; on the other side Arabia. It is difficult of approach from Palestine and Phenicia, but easy from Arabia Nabatæa.

There are three oases, or fertile spots in the desert; the first by Abydus, the second by the Lake Mœris, and the third by the oracle of Ammon. At Syene there is a well into which the sun shines vertically, throwing no shadow, on the longest day of summer, showing the latitude of the city. The Egyptians were, at an early time, very skilful in astronomy; they did not divide the year by lunar months, but by the sun, making it consist of twelve months, each of thirty days, with five days over; and when the extra hours amounted to a whole day they added one to the length of the year. They learned their astronomy from Hermes.

The palm-tree bears fruit in the Thebaid only. The Heracleotic nome is the best cultivated, and there only the olive grows in the fields; in the other parts of Egypt it is confined to the gardens. The *biblus* grows in the lakes and marshes of the Delta; the better kind is called the hieratic biblus [because used in making the sacred books]; it is a naked rush, having a feathery head.

Philadelphus is said first to have opened the road from Coptos to Berenice, to reach the Red Sea without the difficult navigation of the upper part of it: he made stations for travellers, whether on foot or on camels. The Ethiopians are armed with bows four cubits long. The more wealthy Egyptians navigate the river in barges, with couches, and awnings over them, πλοια θαλαμηγα, σκαφαι θαλαμηγαι; they are made of the plant called κυαμος [probably of wicker work?].

There is an accurate representation of the Nilometer of Elephantine in the Hieroglyphics of the Egyptian Society, which agrees with Strabo's description.

The determination of the latitude by means of the sun's shadow is always open to an error of sixteen miles, or 15' 45" of a degree, which is the measure of the sun's semidiameter at the summer solstice; as, whether the sun's centre or edge be vertical, in either case no shadow is thrown. M. Nouet, of the Institut de l'Egypte, found the latitude of Syene 24° 8' 6". The sun's northern declination on the summer solstice, according to Vince's Solar Tables, was 23° 45', B.C. 200, and 23° 50', B.C. 850, the first of which differs twenty miles, the second fifteen; either of these I should quote as a proof of the accuracy of Egyptian observations. And as it is most probable that the observations made at Syene were made at the earlier time, or before the Ethiopian invasion, it would be difficult to deny a very great degree of accuracy to this Egyptian *zenith sector*; for, adding the sun's semidiameter to its declination, we have at that time 24° 5' 45" as the latitude of the most northerly well down which the northern edge of the sun would just shine vertically; a degree of accuracy, however, which must be considered accidental. We see that the use of a leap year, or of an intercalary day on every fourth year, was introduced before the time of Strabo.

The remark that the most easy approach to Egypt from the east was through Arabia Nabatæa is very important, as it explains why the Jews took that apparently roundabout path in their journey out of Egypt. As the desert range of sand hills which stopped their direct march to Palestine runs down to the eastern head of the Red Sea, it was probably in that pass, between the mountain and the sea, that the Egyptian army was drowned: and this is the only route that can be assigned consistently with their passing through Pihahiroth, which was between Magdolus and the Red Sea (Exodus xiv. 2). Their path was nearly southward, whereas commentators who have thought their path was toward the northeast have been obliged to create a second town of the name of Magdolus, or Migdol, on the west of the head of the Red Sea. The enquiry with respect to this interesting march should be, by what route an army would most easily march from Egypt to Palestine, with an enemy in the rear: Strabo answers the question, though Cambyses and Alexander marched by the coast of the Mediterranean sea; but then they both entered Egypt as conquerors, without fear of the opposing army, and took the shortest way, and indeed the precautions which Cambyses took to provide his army with water during the march would prove it a very unsuitable route for a retreat.

Although Egypt is defined as the country watered by the Nile, below the lesser cataract, the term originally was confined to Lower Egypt: thus Strabo says that the palm is barren in all Egypt, but bears fruit in the Thebaid.

Herodotus says that Sesostris was the only Egyptian king that reigned over Ethiopia; did he not mean that he was the only king of Lower Egypt who reigned over Upper Egypt?

Hesiod says that Memnon was king of Ethiopia; did he not mean king of the Thebaid? which we know, from later writers, was the case.

In the first book of Pliny, which contains the subjects of the following books, we find, lib. v. cap. 9, "*Ægypti et Thebaidis*," the Thebaid not being included in Egypt; although he afterwards calls the whole country Egypt.

M. Letrone quotes a Greek inscription in the museum of Verona, with the words The Greeks of the Delta of Egypt, and of the Thebaic nome.

Diodorus says that the Egyptian literature, hieroglyphics, and civilization were natives of Ethiopia; did he not merely mean that Lower Egypt was indebted to Upper Egypt for these advantages?

TACITUS.

GERMANICUS ascended the Nile from the city Canopus. The Spartans built it in honour of Canopus their pilot, whom they buried there, when Menelaus returning to Greece was carried by sea and land to Libya. The next mouth of the Nile is that dedicated to Hercules, who, the natives say, was born among them in a very early age, and whose name they give to those who equal him in valour. Then he (Germanicus) visited the remains of old Thebes, and Egyptian letters were yet remaining on the buildings, recounting the former opulence: and one, who was ordered by the elder priests to interpret his native tongue, related that formerly there dwelt there 700,000 men of the military age; and that with that army King Rhamses, when he had conquered Libya, Ethiopia, the Medes, Persians, Bactrians, and Scythia, held subject the country peopled by the Surians, Armenians, and the neighbouring Cappadocians, and also Bithynia, and Lycia to the coast. He also read the tributes imposed upon these nations, the weight of silver and gold, the number of chariots and horses, and the gifts to the temples of ivory and scents, and what quantity of grain and utensils each nation paid, which were not less magnificent than are now raised by the violence of the Parthians, or by the Roman power. But Germanicus also gave his attention to other wonders, of which the chief were, the stone statue of Memnon, which utters the sound of a voice when struck by the rays of the sun; and the pyramids, built like mountains in the desert by the rivalry and wealth of kings;

and the lake, dug out of the ground to receive the overflowing Nile.—*Annal.* lib. ii.

Germanicus visited Egypt about B.C. 25. The king here mentioned is evidently Rameses II., or the Great; and this is the most authentic account of his conquests that we possess. By comparison with those of Sesostris, as mentioned by Herodotus, we see that the conquests of Rameses extended much further eastward, while Sesostris marched into Thrace, a country which Rameses does not seem to have invaded.

PAUSANIAS.

Lib. i. 42. THE colossus of the Egyptians at Thebes, beyond the Nile and not far from that place which is called the Syringes, appeared to me much more wonderful: for there is even now in this place the statue of a man sitting, which the vulgar call the monument of Memnon. This statue, they say, came from Ethiopia to Egypt, and as far as to Susa. The Thebans, indeed, deny that it is the monument of Memnon, and assert that it is the statue of one of their natives called Phamenophes. I have likewise heard it asserted that it is the statue of Sesostris, which Cambyses dismembered; and even now the upper part, from the head to the middle of the body, lies on the ground, and the remaining part is yet in a sitting posture; and every day when the sun rises it utters a sound similar to that which is produced by the breaking of a harp string.

Lib. x. 31. At Delphos, in a picture representing some of the heroes of the Trojan War, is Memnon, and near him is a naked Ethiopian boy, because Memnon was king of the Ethiopians; but he came to Troy not from Ethiopia but from Susa, a Persian city, and from the river Choaspes, having conquered the cities between Susa and the Choaspes.

Lib. i. 33. The most just men inhabit the city called Meroë, and the plain of Ethiopia; they show the Table of the Sun, and have no river or sea except the Nile; but there are other Ethiopians who dwell near the Mauri.

At Erythræa is a statue of Minerva sailing upon a raft of wood, an exact representation of an Egyptian statue.

The syringes or tunnels, mentioned above, are evidently the tombs of the kings excavated in the hills near Thebes, mentioned in page 62. The remark that Memnon, Amenophis, and Sesostris are different persons is very important; the word Memnon, which is a Greek corruption of Miamon or Amonmai, was a prenomen belonging to the family of Rameses, and never applied to Amenothph except in the case of this celebrated musical statue; and in this instance the Thebans pointed out the mistake to Pausanias. Memnon, or Rameses V., who lived at the time of the Trojan War, is confounded by Pausanias with Memnon, or Rameses II., who built the palace called the Memnonium at Thebes, and another of the same name at Abydus, and who is said to have conquered Persia, and to have built the palace at Susa also called the Memnonium. Rameses II. has by moderns been confounded with Sesostris; but Herodotus is careful to distinguish between them, and points out (lib. ii. 106) that the trophies of Sesostris, erected in Asia Minor, have been sometimes erroneously supposed to be those of Memnon.

PLINY.

Lib. xxxvi. 13. ABOUT Syene there is quarried Thebic syenite, which was before called *pyropœcilon*. 14. Formerly the kings made beams of it in rivalry with one other, calling them obelisks, dedicated to the god the Sun, in representation of its rays, as the Egyptian name signified.

Mestres, who reigned in the city of the Sun [Thebes?] was the first who made one, being ordered in a dream; and this is written upon it, for the carving and figures which we see upon it are the Egyptian letters. Afterwards other kings in the same city made others; Sothis made four, each of forty-eight cubits in length, and Ramises, who was reigning when Troy was taken, one of forty cubits. There are two others, one by Smarres and the other by Eraphius, without inscriptions, of forty-eight cubits. Ptolemy Philadelphus set up one at Alexandria, which king Nectabis had made (*purum*) plain, without inscription.

That obelisk which Divus Augustus set up in the Great Circus was cut by Semneserteus, who was king when Pythagoras was in Egypt; it is of one hundred and twenty-five feet and three quarters, beside the base, of the same stone: but that which is in the Campus Martius, nine feet less, is by Sesostris. They are both carved, and contain the interpretation of the nature of things according to the philosophy of the Egyptians.

15. A third at Rome, in the Vatican Circus, of the princes Caius and Nero, is the only one made in imitation of that which Nuncoreus, the son of Sesostris, had made; and there also remains another of one hundred cubits, which that king dedicated on his recovery from blindness.

17. But the Sphinx is more worth mention than these [the pyramids]; it is like the sylvan deity of the neighbourhood. They think that Amasis the king is buried in it, and wish it to be considered as transported there; but it is carved out of the natural rock, and polished.

19. There is yet remaining in Egypt in the Heracleopolite nome the first labyrinth that was made, it is said four thousand six hundred years ago, by king Petesuccus, or Tithoes, although Herodotus says that it was all the work of the last Psammetichus : various reasons are given for its being built; Demoteles says that it was the palace of Motherudes, Syceas that it was the sepulchre of Mœris.

Nectabis lived five hundred years before Alexander the Great [evidently a mistake for fifty years, or B. C. 360].

Lib. v. 11. When Amasis was king, Egypt had twenty thousand cities; among others was Coptos, the emporium for Indian and Arabian merchandize, Abydus, celebrated for the palace of Memnon and temple of Osiris, &c.

Lib. v. 9. Egypt was divided into three parts; 1st. The Thebaid, or Upper Egypt, reaching from the lesser cataract till the mountains close upon the Nile a little below Lycopolis. 2d. A small district, being the eastern half of the Delta, including Pharbæthus, Bubastus, Sethrium, and Tanis. 3d. The large remaining district, including Memphis, Sais, &c.

Lib. vi. 35. Ethiopia was broken down by the wars with the Egyptians, alternately ruling and being ruled; but was powerful till the time of the Trojan War, when Memnon was king; and that it ruled over Syria and our coast, in the time of King Cepheus, is known from the fables of Andromeda. The name of Queen Candace descended to their queens for many years.

Lib. xxxiii. 15. Esubopes, king of Colchis, had rooms of gold, with beams, columns, and pilastres of silver, which he obtained on the defeat of Sesostris, king of Egypt, who was so proud that he was used to ride in triumph with conquered kings linked to his chariot.

Lib. vi. 33. Sesostris, king of Egypt, first thought of making a navigable canal from the Nile in the Delta to the Red Sea; afterwards Darius, king of the Persians; and then Ptolemy: the last made a canal one hundred feet wide, forty feet deep, and thirty-seven miles and a half long, as far as the bitter fountains.

34. Juba [who wrote the history of Arabia] says that the people on the banks of the Nile, from Syene to Meroë, were not Ethiopians but Arabs; and that the City of the Sun [Heliopolis], near Memphis in Egypt, was founded by Arabs [probably the Shepherd kings of Manetho].

Lib. vi. 26. [The route to India]. From Alexandria to the city Juliopolis is two miles, thence they sail up the Nile to Coptos for three hundred and three miles, which, when the Etesian winds blow, is performed in twelve days: from Coptos the journey is on camels, with houses placed for the sake of watering: the first is called Hydreuma, thirty-two miles from Coptos; the second is a day's journey further, in the mountains; the third at another Hydreuma, ninety-five miles from Coptos; then upon the mountain; then to the Hydreuma Apollinis, one hundred and eighty-four miles from Coptos; then again upon the mountain; then to the new Hydreuma, two hundred and thirty-three miles from Coptos; there is also an old Hydreuma, called the Troglodytic, where the guard is stationed, four miles from the new Hydreuma; thence to the city Berenice, where is the port of the Red Sea, two hundred and fifty-eight miles from Coptos; but because the greater part of the journey is performed by night, and the day is spent at the stations, the whole journey from Coptos to Berenice is finished on the twelfth day. The voyage may be begun in the middle of summer, before the true heliacal rising (*ortus*) of the dog-star [5 June], or at latest, immediately after the apparent heliacal rising (*exortus*) [18 July] : on about the thirtieth day they reach Ocelis in Arabia, or Canes in the Incense country. There is also a third port, called Muza, which the Indian trade does not touch at, but is only used by the merchants of incense and Arabian scents. Inland there is a city, of which the palace is called Saphar [possibly Sabtah, Gen. x.], and another city, Save [probably Sheba, Gen. x.]. For those who are going to India, it is best to start from Ocelis, whence with the wind Hippalus they reach Muzirim, the nearest emporium of India, in forty days. . . . &c. They sail back from India with the wind Volturnus, in the beginning of the Egyptian month Tybi, our December; or perhaps before the sixth day of the Egyptian month Mechir, that is before the ides of January; so they return in the same year.

Lib. vi. 34. At Berenice, on the day of the solstice [the 21st of June], on the sixth hour [at mid-day], the sun throws no shadow [the latitude of the place is therefore about 23° 45' north]. At Ptolemais and the Trogloditic Berenice, on the forty-fifth day before and after the solstice, the sun throws no shadow at noon [hence the latitude is 16° 55'], and these places are six hundred and two *millia passuum* from the former Berenice; and by this measure, and the unerring theory of the sun's shadow, Eratosthenes determined the size of the earth [making a degree of latitude equal eighty-nine *millia passuum*]. Five days voyage from Ptolemais is Aduliton, a city built by the Egyptian deserters. Ten days rowing, further south, is the port of Isis, near which are stone pillars, with unknown letters upon them [probably hieroglyphical inscriptions]; and this is the furthest point to which Sesostris led his army.

Lib. ii. 75. At Meroë the sun throws no shadow at noon when it is in the eighteenth degree of Taurus, or fourteenth of Leo [hence it was in latitude 16° 55′].

The hieroglyphics on the obelisks at Rome do not altogether confirm this account of Pliny: that in the Piazza del Popolo, from the Circus Maximus, bears the name of Thothmosis IV.; it has on it some smaller names, evidently a later addition, which the engravings do not give accurately enough to depend upon, but they appear to be of Rameses; if this be the fact, it will apologize for Ammianus Marcellinus, who pretends to give a translation of the inscription, and says that it was in honour of Rameses. That in the Campus Martius (on Monte Citorio) has the name of Psammetichus. That of the Vatican Circus has no hieroglyphics upon it and so may possibly be an imitation, but being of syenite is no doubt Egyptian.

· Thus the kings mentioned by Pliny, and identified with those of Manetho, are as follows:

Mestres.	Misaphris, Thothmosis I.
Amasis, of the Sphinx.	Thothmosis IV.
Sothis.	Sethos, Rameses II.
Ramises, Trojan war.	Rameses V.
Amasis.	Amosis of Sais.
Psammetichus.	Psammetichus of Sais.
Semneserteus.	Psammetichus I.
Nectabis.	Nectanebo.
Eraphius.	Vaphris, or Hophra.

Those identified with the names in Herodotus are
  Mœris.   Mœris.
  Nuncoreus, son of Sesostris.   Phero, son of Sesostris.

If we could identify Nuncoreus with any one of Manetho's kings, it would give us Pliny's authority for which was Sesostris; but unfortunately this is not easy: we may strike off the first letter, because all kings' names in the enchorial writing begin with an N, and the hieroglyphical name Darius is found to begin with an N; but even then Uncoreus is not near enough to Osorkon for us to consider them the same name.

The account of the mercantile route to India is beautifully clear; the overland journey from Coptos to Berenice is also detailed in the Itinerary of Antoninus, where, however, it is called two hundred and sixty-six *milliapassuum*, instead of two hundred and forty-eight. The 16th July is correctly considered the latest day on which a slow-sailing vessel should leave Berenice to reach the coast of Malabar at the end of seventy days, by the help of the trade-wind, which now blows in that direction till near the end of September, and then changing, would bring the same vessel home again in the months of November and December. The particular route from Coptos to Berenice was first opened by the Ptolemies, when the Arabs had gained possession of Ethiopia, before which time the trade went still further up the Nile to Meroë, the navigation of the Nile being found much more easy than that of the Red Sea; indeed the long overland journey upon camels to Berenice was preferred to the shorter journey to Cosseir, because the latter would have lengthened the voyage of the Red Sea.

Thus we have seen that at different times the routes from the Mediteranean to the Red Sea have varied considerably: the earliest known was by Coptos and Cosseir, in the reigns of Amunmaithor II., and Osirtesen II., before the route through Ethiopia was opened: after the reign of Misaphris (Thothmosis I.), when Egypt and Ethiopia were under one king, it is probable that they took advantage of the more easy navigation of the Nile for a greater distance, and Cosseir was deserted for a port in Ethiopia. When the independence of Memphis interrupted this inland navigation, the merchants went by Petra to Jerusalem and Tyre, and Sesostris, perhaps with a view to bring the trade through his dominions, proposed to cut a canal from the Red Sea to the Pelusian branch of the Nile. What route was used under the prosperous reigns of the kings of Sais is not evident, but probably the old route, from Coptos to Cosseir, as their power over Ethiopia was weak. On the Persian conquest, when Upper Egypt was ruined by the fury of the conquerors, Darius again began to cut the canal in the Delta: and lastly under the Ptolemies, when all Egypt was quiet and prosperous, the passage of the Nile was again free, and Philadelphus opened the new route from Coptos to Berenice.

VALERIUS FLACCUS.

You here see the beginning of the Colchian nation; how king Sesostris brought war upon the Getæ; how, frightened by the slaughter of his troops, he led some of them back to Thebes, and to their native river, and left some of them in the fields of Phasis, and ordered them to be called Colchians.—*Argonaut.* lib. v. 418.

We have seen that Pliny mentions this defeat of Sesostris by the Getæ; and though Herodotus does not mention any defeat, these

passages are quite consistent with his account of the king marching through Palestine to Thrace, and leaving some of his troops behind, who settled in Colchis; Herodotus adds that the Colchians and Egyptians spoke the same language.

HOMER.

Il. ix. 381. ACHILLES says that no rewards would make him change his mind. " Not the wealth of Egyptian Thebes, where treasures are most numerous in the houses, where there are one hundred gates, and out of each of these, two hundred warriors issue with chariots and horses."

Menelaus, after his return from Troy, visited Ethiopia and Egypt (Od. iv. 84): he was hospitably received at Thebes by Polybus and his wife Alcandra, who gave to him and Helen (iv. 126), among other gifts, ten talents of gold.

Polydamna, the wife of Thōn (iv. 228), gave to Helen some valuable medicines; she was an Egyptian, and all Egyptians are skilful in medicine, being of the race of Pæeon.

Il. xxiii. 206. Iris says that she is going to the land of the Ethiopians, who are sacrificing hecatombs to the immortal gods.

Od. xi. 521. Memnon was eminent for his beauty.

These passages in Homer are principally worth notice from the importance attached, by the authors who followed him, to every thing that he wrote: for, whatever weight we should allow to Homer's authority in those narrative parts of his work which are more particularly historical, and relate to the country with which the writer was probably well acquainted, less must be thought due to Menelaus's narration of his travels in Egypt, a country which it is evident that Homer had never visited. Nevertheless, the authors who succeeded him thought his narrative of such importance that when Manetho, in arranging the chronology of his history, found that Thuoris reigned at Thebes such a number of generations back [*i.e.* B.C. 900], he adds, this is the Polybus of Homer; and when Diodorus found that, at the same time, Sais was ruled over by Ketna, he immediately fixed upon him for the Proteus of Homer; and, indeed, Herodotus gives no name to the king whom he considered contemporary with the Trojan War, he only calls him Proteus. Homer, however, does not call them kings.

More modern travellers, from Diodorus Siculus to the present time, knowing that Thebes had never been a walled city, have conjectured that the epithet " with its hundred gates," alluded to its porticoes; but the above passage is explicit; Homer must have thought it a walled city.

HESIOD.

MEMNON, with the brazen helmet, the king of the Ethiopians, was the son of Tithon and Aurora.—*Theogony*.

This passage is valuable as showing that, by the early Greeks, Upper Egypt was included in the word Ethiopia.

PLUTARCH.

TECHNATIS, the father of Bacchoris, is said, when leading an army against the Arabs, to have used the simple food which fell in his way, and to have slept so soundly upon it that he set up at Thebes a column, on which he wrote a curse against Meines the king who had taught the Egyptians the luxury of cooking.

The great deeds of Sesostris were still celebrated in Egypt.

The dog-star was called Sothis by the Egyptians.—*De Isid. &c.*

And hence the term Sothic year, which was founded upon sidereal observations, from which alone they could have learnt that the year did not contain an exact number of days. For these observations large stars, such as the dog-star, alone were suitable, before the invention of glasses. Other nations, whose year was founded upon the more obvious observations of the sun, found their calendar constantly too erroneous for use, and set it right by intercalary days, which were not like our 29th of February recurring by a fixed rule, but added occasionally when found necessary.

The name of Sesostris had acquired an heroic celebrity, like that of Charlemagne; the deeds of many of the early kings were attributed to him, and some of the later kings may have assumed this name: and hence the difficulty of determining which real king was meant by authors who spoke of Sesostris.

AMMIANUS MARCELLINUS.

" THEBES was a city built in the early ages, celebrated for its approaches through one hundred gates; this city the Carthaginian generals sacked (*oppressére*) by a sudden irruption, when Carthage was first extending its power; it was then repaired, and afterwards attacked by Cambyses, king of the Persians."

This may have been at any time between B.C. 500 and B.C. 900.

XENOPHON.

CYRUS conquered the Greeks in Asia Minor, and passing over the sea subdued the Cyprians and Egyptians.—*Cyropædia,* lib. i.

QUINTUS CURTIUS.

ALEXANDER entered Egypt from Gaza, along the coast, to Pelusium, and then went up the Nile to Memphis, and " the interior." When he had made himself master of the country, always endeavouring to avoid disturbing the prejudices of the Egyptians (" *ita ut nihil ex patrio Ægyptiorum more mutaret*"), he set off for the oracle of Jupiter Ammon, going by water to the lake Mareotis, [of Mœris] then marching for four days through the desert to the oasis. The image of the god was peculiar, being half man and half ram, divided at the waist. On his return he chose a site for his new city, Alexandria. He had not leisure to visit Ethiopia nor the palace of Tithonian Memnon [Thebes], to which his curiosity in regard to antiquities led him.

Among the doubtful accounts of where was the oasis of Ammon, this is the one most entitled to credit; Belzoni found ruins in the most northerly oasis at about the latitude of Memphis, at a distance agreeing with this account. Herodotus, however, (see page 22) distinctly says that the oasis of Ammon was a seven days march from Thebes, meaning the great oasis.

PORPHYRY,

(An author of the age of Dioclesian, quoted in Scaliger's Eusebius.)

"ALEXANDER the Macedonian died in the 114th Olympiad, after a reign of twelve years in the whole; and was succeeded in his kingdom by Aridæus, whose name was changed to Philip, being brother to Alexander by another mother, for he was the son of Philip by Philinna of Larissa; and, after a reign of seven years, he was killed in Macedonia by Polysperchon the son of Antipater.

" Now Ptolemy the son of Arsinoë and of Lagus, after one year of this reign, by an appointment derived from Philip, was sent as a satrap into Egypt, which he governed in this capacity for seventeen years, and afterwards with royal authority for twenty-three years; so that the number of all the years of his government, to the time of his death, became forty; but since he retired from the government two years before in favour of his son Ptolemy Philadelphus, and considered himself as a subject of his son, who had been crowned in his place, the years of this first Ptolemy, called Soter, are reckoned, not forty, but thirty-eight only. He was succeeded by his son, surnamed as already mentioned, Philadelphus, who reigned two years during his father's life-time, and thirty [six] afterwards, so that his whole reign occupied, like his father's, thirty-eight years.

" In the third place, the throne was ascended by Ptolemy surnamed Euergetes, who reigned twenty-five years.

" In the fourth, by Ptolemy called Philopater, whose reign was in the whole seventeen years.

" After him, the fifth Ptolemy was surnamed Epiphanes, and reigned twenty-four years.

"Epiphanes had two sons, both named Ptolemy, who reigned after him, the elder was surnamed Philometer, and the younger Euergetes the Second; their reigns together occupy a period of sixty-four years.

"We have placed this as a single number, because, as they were at variance with each other and reigned alternately, the dates were necessarily confounded: for Philometer first reigned eleven years alone; but, when Antiochus made war upon Egypt and deprived him of his crown, the Alexandrians committed the government to the charge of his younger brother, and, having driven back Antiochus, set Philometer at liberty. They then numbered the year the [twelfth] of Philometer and the first of Euergetes; and this system was continued till the seventeenth, but from the eighteenth forwards the years are attributed to Philometer alone, for the elder, having been expelled from his kingdom by the younger, was restored by the Romans; and he retained the crown of Egypt, leaving his brother the dominion of Libya, and continued to reign alone for eighteen years. He died in Syria, having conquered that country. Euergetes being then recalled from Cyrene and proclaimed king, continued to number the years of his reign from his first accession to the crown; so that, having reigned [twenty-nine] years after the death of his brother, he extended his dates to fifty-four, for the thirty-sixth year of Philometer, which should have been called his first, he determined to make the twenty-fifth. In the whole, therefore, we have sixty-four; first, thirty-five of Philometer, and the remainder of Euergetes: but the subdivision may lead to confusion.

"Now Ptolemy Euergetes the Second had two sons, called Ptolemy, by Cleopatra; the elder Soter, and the younger [Alexander]. The elder was proclaimed king by his mother: and, appearing to be obsequious to her wishes, he was beloved for a certain time; but when, in the tenth year of his reign, he put to death the friends of his parents, he was deposed by his mother for his cruelty, and driven as a fugitive into Cyprus. The mother then sent for her younger son from Pelusium, and proclaimed him sovereign together with herself; so that they reigned in common, the dates of public acts being referred to both, and the year was called the eleventh of Cleopatra and the eighth of Ptolemy Alexander, comprehending the time as a part of his reign which began with the fourth year of his brother, during which he reigned in Cyprus: and this custom continued during the whole of the life of Cleopatra, but after her death the epoch of Alexander alone was employed; and though he actually held the sceptre for eighteen years only, from the time of his return to Alexandria, he appears in his public records as having reigned twenty-six. In his nineteenth year, having quarrelled with his troops, he went out into the country, in order to raise a force to control them; but they pursuing him, under the command of Tyrrhus, a relation of the royal family, engaged him by sea, and compelled him to fly with his wife and daughter to Myræ, a city of Lycia; whence crossing over to Cyprus, and being attacked by Chæreas, who had the command of the hostile fleet, he was killed in battle.

" The Alexandrians, after his flight, sent an embassy to the elder Ptolemy, Soter [or Lathurus], inviting him back from Cyprus, to take possession of the kingdom. During the seven years and six months that he survived after his return, the whole time that had elapsed since the death of his father was attributed to his reign: so that the number of years became thirty-five and six months, of which, however, only seventeen and six months properly belong to him, in the two separate portions of his reign: while the second brother, Alexander, had reigned eighteen in the intermediate time: and although these could not be effaced from the annals, they suppressed them as far as it was in their power, since he had offended them by some alliance with the Jews. They do not therefore reckon these years separately, but attribute the whole thirty-six to the elder brother, omitting again to assign to Cleopatra, the daughter of the elder and wife of the younger brother, who took possession of the government after her father's death, the six months that she reigned, which were a part of the thirty-sixth year. Nor did they distinguish, by the name of the Alexander that succeeded her, the nineteen days that he retained the crown. This Alexander was the son of the younger brother, Ptolemy Alexander, and the step-son of Cleopatra; he was residing at Rome, and the Egyptian dynasty failing of male heirs, he came by invitation to Alexandria, and married this same Cleopatra [his step-mother]; and, having deprived her by force of her authority, he put her to death after nineteen days, and was himself killed in the gymnasium, by the guards, whom his barbarity had disgusted.

"Alexander the Second was succeeded by Ptolemy who was called Neus Dionysus, or the young Bacchus, the son of Ptolemy Soter and the brother of the Cleopatra last mentioned: his reign continued for twenty-nine years.

"His daughter Cleopatra was the last of the family of the Lagidæ, and the years assigned to her reign are twenty-two. Neither did these different reigns fill up the whole series of years from beginning to end in a regular order, but several of them were intermixed. For in the time of Dionysus, three years are attributed to his two daughters, Cleopatra Tryphæna, and Berenice, a year conjointly, and two years, after the death of Cleopatra Tryphæna, to Berenice alone; because in this interval Ptolemy was gone to Rome, and was spending his time there, while his daughters, as if he were not about to return, took possession of the government for themselves, Berenice having also called in to a share of her dominion some men who were her relations; until Ptolemy, returning from Rome, and forgetting the indulgence due to a daughter, took offence at her conduct and deprived her of life.

" The first years of the reign of his successor Cleopatra were also referred to her in common with her elder brother Ptolemy, and the following to other persons, for this reason: Ptolemy Neus Dionysus [or Auletes], left at his death four children, two Ptolemies, and Cleopatra, and Arsinoë, appointing as his successors his two elder children, Ptolemy and Cleopatra; they were considered as joint sovereigns for four years, and would have remained so, but that Ptolemy, having departed from his father's commands and resolved to keep the whole power in his own hands, it was his fate to be slain in a sea-fight near the coasts of Egypt, by Julius Cæsar, who took part with Cleopatra.

" After the destruction of this Ptolemy, Cleopatra's younger brother, also called Ptolemy, was placed on the throne with his sister by Cæsar's decree, and the year was called the fifth of Cleopatra and the first of Ptolemy; and this custom continued till his death, for two more years. But when he had been destroyed by the arts of Cleopatra, in his fourth year and in the eighth of his sister, the subsequent years were distinguished by the name of Cleopatra alone, as far as fifteen. The sixteenth was named also the first, since, after the death of Lysimachus king of Chalcis in Syria, the Autocrator Mark Antony gave Chalcis and all the neighbouring country to Cleopatra; and from this time the remaining years of her reign, as far as the twenty-second which was the last, were reckoned in the same manner, with an additional number, the twenty-second having been called also the seventh [as the Armenian has very properly read for the twenty-seventh].

"From Cleopatra the government devolved to Octavius Cæsar, called also Augustus, who overcame the power of Egypt in the battle of Actium, the second year of the 184th Olympiad. And from the first year of the 111th Olympiad, when Aridæus Philippus [or rather Alexander], the son of Philip, took possession of the government, to the second of the 184th, there are seventy-three Olympiads and a year, or two hundred and ninety-three years; and so many are the years of the sovereigns that reigned in Alexandria to the time of the death of Cleopatra."—Dr. Young's Translation.

On the Egyptian Year.

HERODOTUS, who is the earliest authority for many subjects connected with Egypt, informs us that in his time three hundred and sixty-five days was thought by the Egyptians to be the true length of the natural year; his words are that " the Egyptians were the first to invent the [true civil] year, adapting it to the twelve parts of the seasons. They assert that these [the twelve seasons] were discovered by means of the stars. They have twelve months of thirty days each, and add five days at the end of each year: and the seasons, which return to the same point at the end of their revolution, always remain parallel with these [civil months]."

The sidereal observation, by which the length of the year was determined, was the noting of the heliacal rising of the stars, and of Sothis, the dog-star, in particular. The day on which the star and sun are in conjunction, when the star cannot be seen, is called the day of the star's *true* heliacal rising; and the first day, after the conjunction, that the star is far enough from the sun to be seen is called the day of its *apparent* heliacal rising, or, shortly, its rising, when it is seen to rise just before sunrise, which in Egypt, in the case of the dog-star, is about the forty-third day after the conjunction.

The rising of the dog-star, which is now in the middle of August, and was in the time of Herodotus in the middle of July (the change being occasioned by the precession of the equinox), was the beginning of the Egyptian natural year, and was celebrated as the time when the waters of the Nile began to rise. It is obvious that the precise day could not be determined with exactness; the clearness of the atmosphere and brightness of the morning twilight might both vary with the weather, and make the rising of the dog-star uncertain, to the extent of three or four days. Hence it would require a course of several years to determine that, upon an average, three hundred and sixty-five days elapsed between two risings of the star: and, as the life of a man would hardly allow more than an observation of forty years' length, it is not probable that, in this way, they should ever have noted the want of our 29th of February, or have ventured, against their preconceived opinions, to pronounce that the year did not contain an exact number of whole days, but three hundred and sixty-five days and a quarter.

If we are right in the explanation of the above passage in Herodotus, we see that, while the civil year contained twelve months and five days, the natural year contained twelve seasons; and this seems to explain the astronomical sculpture on the Memnonium, part of which is drawn on Plate VI. from Mr. Wilkinson's *Materia Hieroglyphica*. The female figure in the boat has over her left hand the word Isis-Sothis, or dog-star, and is understood to represent that star rising heliacally; above is the name of the first month in the year, Thoth; the man in the other boat is another constellation rising heliacally, probably the Bull, but the name is not understood; the group of stars represents the constellation, and the seven smaller stars may be the Pleiades; the month above is the last month in the year, Mesore. The two stars in the middle may be the Twins, above each of which is the word Gods, in the dual, and in the same sense the word Kings in the dual accompanies the Twins in the Ptolemaic Zodiac at Dendera. In the order of their right ascension, the stars would stand—the Pleiades, Sothis, Gemini; yet in the order of their heliacal rising, which is undoubtedly what

THE EGYPTIAN YEAR. 113

is here alluded to, they would follow as above-mentioned, the Pleiades, Gemini, Sothis. We have here to remark, that we do not see in the sculpture the five days, which in the civil year were inserted between the months Mesore and Thoth; hence I conclude that the natural portions of the seasons are here spoken of, and not the civil months.

The ZODIAC of DENDERA, for which see the plates to Denon's Voyage, quite confirms this interpretation of the figures on the Memnonium: in the Zodiac the year is divided into two halves, and the principal astronomical phenomena in the latter half of the year, from February to July inclusive, may be thus described:

The sun in Aquarius: among other figures, a man with a vase in each hand, pouring out water; on his head is a bunch of flowers, the hieroglyphic for *Greek* or *foreign*, being the character for *Greek* in the last line of the Rosetta stone, which here seems to denote that it is in foreign lands only that this is the rainy season.

The sun in Pisces: two fishes, and other figures.

The sun in Aries: a ram lying down, and other figures.

The sun in Taurus: a bull and other figures.

The sun in Gemini: two figures, holding hands, one has a tiger's head.

Next follows, at an interval of a month and a half, or forty-five days after the constellation Taurus, the male figure in a boat of our Plate VI., and therefore quite at the right time for the apparent heliacal rising of the Bull, that constellation being here represented by the Egyptian figure.

The sun in Cancer: a cow lying down in a boat. This is the only one of the twelve signs which is represented by an Egyptian figure, the other eleven are all Greek. It would seem as if, from the importance attached to the rising of the dog-star in Egypt, this month was not marked by the conjunction of the Sun and Cancer, but by that heliacal rising: the cow denotes Isis.

Half a month further we have two figures in a boat, one a man, the dog-star, the other a woman, Isis, crowned as in Plate VI., pouring out water from a vase in each hand, to denote the overflowing of the Nile, which took place at this time: the whole represents the apparent heliacal rising of the dog-star, and it follows forty-five days after the sun was in Gemini. We shall see, when we come to the Mythology, that Isis was placed in the constellation Sirius.

Here the year ends, and then follows Leo; and half a month before Libra is a woman holding an ear of bearded wheat, to denote the harvest. The whole is a description of the natural year, there is no mention of civil months; at this time they were quite aware that the civil year did not coincide with the astronomical phenomena. As far as already described it is a Greek Zodiac; underneath it there is a second row of figures, of Egyptian gods in boats, which seems intended to represent the Egyptian division of the year by the heliacal rising of the constellations; there are nineteen boats or constellations in each half-year:—but to return to the subject of the Egyptian year.

The names of the months were—

1. Thoth.
2. Paophi.
3. Athyr.
4. Chœac.
5. Tybi.
6. Mechir.
7. Phamenoth.
8. Pharmuthi.
9. Pachon.
10. Payni.
11. Epiphi.
12. Mesore.
13. Five days.

Before Diodorus Siculus visited Egypt they had made further advances in astronomy, had discovered new modes of observing, and, by them, had learned more accurately the true length of the

THE EGYPTIAN YEAR.

natural year: he says that they considered it three hundred and sixty-five days and a quarter (see page 30). Ptolemy explains how this was learned, by the observations of Hipparchus and himself.

Hipparchus made his observations at Alexandria by means of a fixed armillary sphere, and noted with it at what time the two sides of the equatorial plane were both illuminated by the sunshine, at which instant the sun was in the equator, and consequently in the equinox.

In the 178th year after the death of Alexander [B. C. 145], the vernal equinox fell on the 27th day of Mechir, on the fifth hour [one hour before noon]; and eighteen years afterwards it fell on the first day of Phamenoth at sun-set, or four days and seven hours later: if these 4 days and 7 hours be divided by 18, the number of years, the quotient will be 5 hours and 43 minutes, showing that the tropical year contained 365 days, 5 hours, and 43 minutes, which is about 6 minutes less than the truth.

In the 463d year after the death of Alexander, Ptolemy made a similar observation, to compare with the first of these, and found the vernal equinox fall on the 7th day of Pachon, one hour after noon, or 70 days and 2 hours later than it had done two hundred and eighty-five years before, making the tropical year consist of 365 days, 5 hours, 54 minutes, or 6 hours wanting a 300th part of a day, as he expresses it, which is about 5 minutes more than the truth.

These observations are curious, as showing the degree of accuracy attained by these astronomers, and are important as proving that they recorded their observations by means of the civil year of 365 days, which of course, when compared with the stars or seasons, was a moveable year.

It was not till the year B.C. 25 that the Romans introduced into

Egypt the Julian method of an intercalary day, and made the civil year consist of 365 days and a quarter; and it was about that time that Egypt was made a Roman province, as we learn from an inscription at the foot of the obelisk on Monte Citorio, quoted by Nibby in his notes to Nardini.

IMP . CAESAR . DIVI . F
AVGVSTVS
PONTIFEX . MAXIMVS
IMP . $\overline{\text{XII}}$. COS . $\overline{\text{XI}}$. TRIB . POT . $\overline{\text{XIV}}$.
AEGYPTO . IN . POTESTATEM
POPVLI . ROMANI . REDACTA
SOLI . DONVM . DEDIT

The astronomers, however, long after this time continued to record their observations by means of the moveable year of 365 days only, as we see by the above observations of Ptolemy.

As soon as it was discovered that the length of the year was 365 days and a quarter, and that the civil year, of 365 days only, was a moveable year, it was naturally remarked that if at any time these two years began at the same day, it would be 1461 years before it so happened again; and this period of four times three hundred and sixty-five and a quarter was called the Great Year or Sothic Period, from Sothis, the name of the dog-star. The subject is thus explained by

CENSORINUS.

In Egypt the year originally consisted of two months; afterwards, by king Ison, it was made to consist of four months; and lastly Arminon lengthened it to thirteen months and five days. Some say that Horus made the year consist of three months.

The Egyptian Great Year was not connected with the moon; the Greeks called it Cynic, and the Latins Canicular, because it began when the dog-star rose upon the first day of Thoth. The civil year had 365 days, without any intercalary day; hence four Egyptian years contained one day less than four natural years; hence the civil year began again at the same day of the natural year after a period of 1461 years.

This year, which is the consulate of Ulpius and Pontianus, is the 1014th from the first Olympiad, the 986th of the era of Nabonnazaru. On this year the first day of the month of Thoth was *ante diem* VII. *Kal. Julii*, and one hundred years ago it was *ante diem* XII. *Kal. August.*, at which time the dog-star rises in Egypt; hence we learn that we are now in the hundredth year of the Egyptian Great Year. The Greeks considered themselves quite as much indebted to the Babylonians as to the Egyptians for their knowledge of astronomy.—*De Die Natali*.

From this we learn that the moveable 1st of Thoth, or new year's day, was, A. C. 140, on the 18th July, and easily find that B. C. 25 it must have been on the 29th of August: and this agrees with what we are told by Egyptian travellers, namely, that the first of Thoth is now on the 10th of September; for, as the Egyptians have used the Julian calendar ever since B. C. 25,—and by Pope Gregory's arrangement our calendar differs from that by 12 days,— our 10th of September, new style, is the same as their 29th of August, old style.

From the above passage in Censorinus we also learn that the former occasion on which the 1st of Thoth coincided with the heliacal rising of the dog-star, or the beginning of the former canicular period, was B. C. 1321 if we neglect the precession of the equinoxes, or B.C. 1285 if it be taken into account, and this enables us to fix with astronomical certainty the time when one very early king reigned.

THEON, as quoted by Larcher in his Notes to Herodotus, calls the first year of the Sothic period the epoch of Menophres, from which we have the curious information that Menophres was king of Egypt B. C. 1321. Unfortunately we cannot identify him, with the certainty we could wish, with any one of Manetho's kings; but if we remark that this name is Men-Hophres, and that in the 26th dynasty we have the name of Hophris or Vaphris, and in the 18th dynasty the name of Mis-Hophris, or Misaphris, the agreement would seem close enough to justify us in quoting this most important information as a proof that we have done right in assigning the date of B. C. 1321 to Misaphris, in the Chart of History. In addition to which we have the authority of Herodotus for Mœris living 900 years before the time when he wrote his history, or about B. C. 1320, making it probable that Misaphris, Menophres, and Mœris are the same king.

We have just seen that, while the natural new year's day, which was a day of rejoicing, as being about the time when the Nile began to rise, was fixed, and was the day on which the dog-star rose apparently heliacally, the civil new year's day moved one day in four years, and made a complete revolution in 1461 years; hence, if we knew on what day of the natural year any one civil year began, we should know at what part of the Sothic period the year spoken of was. And so also the reverse,—if we are told on what day of a civil month any astronomical phenomenon happened, we should know what year of the Sothic period was spoken of; and, as we know that the Sothic period began B. C. 1321, we should know how long before our era the year was.

This being the case, if the words Thoth and Mesore, in Plate VI., are meant for the moveable civil months, that sculpture conveys a date, for the heliacal rising of the dog-star is mentioned in connection with the month of Thoth. And this is the view taken of it by several learned writers on Egyptian antiquities; they understand the sculpture to mean, that in the year that it was made the heliacal rising of the dog-star coincided with the moveable 1st of Thoth; and hence they correctly draw the conclusion that Rameses II., in whose reign it was made, lived B.C. 1321, or rather, taking into account the precession of the equinoxes, B. C. 1285.

But, before the sculpture is considered as proving this important fact, it is necessary that we should be shown that the civil year of 365 days is here spoken of; we must be shown in Plate VI. the five intercalary days which came between these two months; and I can by no means agree to consider, with Mr. Wilkinson, that five out of the seven stars, over the head of the male figure, are those five days; and even if the months mentioned in the sculpture be understood to be the months of the civil year, we still have the information of Herodotus, that even in his days, centuries after the sculpture was made, they thought the sidereal year contained 365 days exactly; they had not yet invented the Sothic period; they had not yet discovered that the 1st of Thoth was moveable, when compared with the astronomical phenomena. Besides, no particular day of the month is mentioned in the sculpture; and, as we are quite without evidence that the Egyptians had attained to any great degree of accuracy in observing the heliacal rising of the stars, an observation which is essentially rude, this sculpture must have but little weight in contradicting the chronology assumed in these pages, according to which Rameses II., the author of this sculpture, lived about B. C. 1050, at which time the dog-star rose heliacally about the 1st day of Athyr.

How early the Egyptians possessed much knowledge of astronomy, it is very difficult to form an opinion. Ptolemy quotes Babylonian observations even as early as B.C. 720, but quotes no Egyptian observations earlier than those of Timocharis, B. C. 300. The Babylonian method of dividing the year was the same as the Egyptian, and can be traced back to the time of Mardoc Empadus, B. C. 720. And the Babylonian astronomers are alluded to in 2 Chron. xxxii. 31, 2 Kings xx. 8, as sending to Jerusalem about the year B.C. 700, to enquire into the phenomenon of the sun's shadow moving backwards upon the dial ten degrees, as a sign to King Hezekiah, which was evidently not observed at Babylon: but then we do not know which nation learned astronomy from the other. That Ptolemy calls the Babylonian months by the Egyptian names proves but little, for he might have translated them. These names we have seen were in use in Egypt in the reign of Rameses II. B. C. 1040; and, indeed, the sculpture of Plate VI. shows that at that early time they noted the heliacal risings of the stars, which is at least 300 years earlier than the first Babylonian observation on record. The Egyptian era of Menophris began B.C. 1321, while the Babylonian era of Nabonassar only began B. C. 747. Herodotus however tells us (lib. ii. 109) that the Babylonians discovered the use of the gnomon and the pole of the earth, without which knowledge the armillary sphere of Hipparchus could not have been constructed nor the true length of the year so nearly determined.

On the Physical Character of the Egyptians.

THAT neither the Egyptians nor their Ethiopian neighbours were Negroes has been so often and so satisfactorily proved that it seems hardly necessary to allude to the opinion: by the paintings in the tombs at Thebes we learn that they were well acquainted with the Negro race, and while these are painted black they are themselves painted of a red colour. There is a considerable difference between the statues which we possess of the kings of Upper Egypt and the mummies, which are all probably far more modern; and neither of these agree with the present race of Egyptians. The portraits of the kings, although sufficiently removed from the Negro, have rather prominent jaws, thick lips, and a broad flattened nose; they have also prominent eyes, a considerable beard, and long hair: of this form of countenance we have numerous specimens in the British Museum. In some of the mummies, the difference from the above-described character is very great; the nose is long and slender and finely arched, the lips thin, and of this the engraving in Mr. Pettigrew's History of Mummies is a good example. Blumenbach, as quoted in Lawrence's Lectures on Physiology, divides the Egyptian mummies into three classes; the first he calls the Ethiopian variety, carefully remarking that by that name he does not mean Negro, but those having a physiognomy similar to that of the Egyptian statues; secondly, the Hindoo or Eastern variety, which agrees closely in physiognomy and bodily structure with the inhabitants of Hindostan; and thirdly, the Berber variety, having loose cheeks, large projecting eyes, and a swollen habit of body. These three subdivisions are all included, by Blumenbach and

Cuvier, in the Caucasian variety of the human race, the group which includes all those nations that have made the great advances in civilization.

Mr. Pettigrew has given the measurements of seventeen mummies, by which it appears that the Egyptians were short in stature, as the average height of the male is 5 feet 3 inches, and of the female 5 feet.

But the mummies which have been examined seem all to belong to the more modern times of Egyptian history; they frequently contain inscriptions in the enchorial language, of which the use cannot be traced earlier than the reign of Psammetichus I.; these inscriptions are usually written on papyrus, which, like the enchorial language, seems to have been first used under the kings of Sais, but not to have become common till the time of the Ptolemies; and some few mummies contain Greek inscriptions. Hence the diversity in the physical character of the mummies is explained; they were probably made at a time when the Egyptians were no longer an unmixed Coptic race; they had been conquered successively by the Arabs of Ethiopia, by the Persians, and by the Greeks, and their physiological character, as well as their language, seems to have been altered by the admixture.

LUCIAN, who lived for some time in Egypt, describes in his Dialogues, philosophy as travelling from the Hindoos to the Ethiopians, and thence to the Egyptians; and ridicules, in the case of Io and Isis, the opinion that the Greek mythology was borrowed from the Egyptian.

In the latter case, all modern research contradicts Lucian's opinion, and proves that the Greeks derived much of their religion and of their art from Egypt: in the former case, there are many slight but curious circumstances which make it probable that civilization, as well as wealth, may have crossed from Hindostan to Ethiopia, by means of the trade-winds, and thence descended the Nile. The excavated temples in the island named by the Portuguese Elephanta, near to Bombay, containing colossal busts of the Hindoo Triad, of which the heads are six feet high, and various mythological sculptures, bear close analogy to the Egyptian works of art. The Egyptian lotus and hooded snake seem to be borrowed from the Hindoos; the sacred snake, basilisk, or asp in each country was a viper of the sub-genus Naja, which has a loose skin under its neck, which it can swell out at will; in which condition it is accurately represented in the hieroglyphical sculptures (see Plate V. fig 54). Cuvier's description of the animal is as follows: " Les *Naja* elargissent en disque la partie de leurs corps la plus voisine de leur tête, en redressant et tirant en avant les côtes qui la soutiennent; leur tête est couverte de grandes plaques." (*Règne Animal*). Cuvier adds that the Egyptian jugglers, by pressing the finger on the nape of the serpent's neck, can put it into a kind of catalepsy, which makes it motionless and stiff, like a rod (see Exodus vii. 9, 12.) The hereditary division of the people into castes, the doctrine of the transmigration of the soul, and the grouping of their deities into triads, also seem to have been common to both countries; and lastly, the anatomists on examining the mummies find that a considerable portion of them partake of the Hindoo physiology, in respect of the skull and the skeleton generally.

On the Mythology of the Egyptians.

HERODOTUS, Diodorus, and Plutarch have given us a few distinct particulars of the Egyptian gods, and we also learn something respecting them from most of the Greek authors who have written about their own mythology. Both Greeks and Romans were in the habit, when they became acquainted with the gods of other countries, of taking it for granted that they were the same as their own under other names, and, consequently, their first and frequently only enquiry was, which was Jupiter, which Juno, &c. This was in many cases a most useless comparison of characters which had nothing in common; but not so in the case of the Egyptians, since we have sufficient evidence that many of the gods of the Greeks were either wholly or partially borrowed from Egypt, which gives an additional interest to inquiries respecting the Egyptian traditions.

The monuments of ancient Egypt are full of pictures of their gods, with inscriptions attached to each figure. These inscriptions are not always perfectly understood, and in general contain little beyond expressions of praise; the information, however, in many cases agrees with what the ancient authors have handed down to us.

According to Diodorus, the Egyptian mythology, together with the hieroglyphics and learning, were natives of Ethiopia; and the sun, moon, and earth were the only gods which were not originally mortal heroes. There were twelve principal gods, and of these eight were the superior, but we do not know which these were. Those most clearly pointed out as reigning upon earth are Osiris and his queen Isis, their son Horus, and his successor Typhon;

and this is the principal group or family mentioned. We are frequently told in which cities they were particularly honoured, for Isis and Osiris were the only divinities which Herodotus found in honour all over Egypt.

Amun-Ra, King of the gods, Lord of heaven, the Great ruler, is well known in the sculptures: his name is literally the Great Sun. He was worshipped more particularly at Thebes, and while that city was the capital of Egypt, Amunmai, or Beloved by Amun, was the favourite title of the kings. He was the Zeus or Jupiter Ammon of the Greeks; he holds in his hands various sceptres, one frequently in the form of a whip; his most usual crown is represented Plate V. fig. 59. A globe was emblematical of him, which is frequently ornamented with an asp or snake, denoting immortality, and with wings, the common emblem of divinity. He sometimes has rams' horns, which were adopted in the portraits of Alexander, who marched through the desert to the temple of Amun-Ra and asserted that he was the son of this god. He is sometimes called Ra, and sometimes Amun, simply. Plate V. fig. 25 and 60 are names of this god, the one phonetic the other symbolic.

Knuphis, Cenubis, or Kneph was probably only another name for this god: he is generally represented with the rams' horns, and other peculiarities of Amun-Ra, and there is an inscription at Syene, of the time of Caracalla, to Jupiter Hammon Cenubis. Strabo also says that Knuphis was worshipped at Elephantine. Plutarch says that, while all the other cities of Egypt were taxed to support the animals which they respectively worshipped, Thebes alone was exempt, because the Thebans worshipped Kneph alone, whom they thought unborn and immortal. All these circumstances are enough to prove that Amun-Ra and Kneph are the same.

Chemmis or Pan is also in his figures in some respects like

Amun-Ra, though upon the whole a very distinct deity. He was worshipped at Mendes, and the goat was sacred to him. The city of Chemmis was called Panopolis by the Greeks, which sufficiently connects his Greek with the Coptic name. The latter was Chem or Ham, being the same with the son of Noah, the great founder of the nation (see page 8), and with the name of the country itself, for ⲬⲎⲙⲓ is the Coptic name of Egypt; hence his importance must have been considerable. He had some of the attributes of Priapus; and Stephanus *De Urbibus*, quoted by the translator of Pausanias, thus describes a statue of Pan: ἐστι δε και του θεου ἀγαλμα μεγα, ὀρθιακον ἐχων το αἰδοιον εἰς ἐπτα δακτυλους· ἐπαιρει τε μαστιγας τῃ δεξιᾳ σελινῃ, ἧς εἰδωλον φασιν εἰναι τον Πανα. We accordingly recognize his figure, holding up the whip in his right hand with his left arm close to his side, and an altar behind him. Diodorus also says, τας εἰκονας αὐτων ἀνατιθεναι τους πλειστους ἐν τοις ἱεροις ἐντεταμενας και τῃ του τραγου φυσει παραπλησιας.

Pthah, Hephaistos, or Vulcan was the great object of worship at Memphis, which explains his importance in the eyes of Herodotus and Diodorus. When Memphis became the capital at which the kings were crowned, Beloved by Pthah became the title of the kings. The sacred bull kept at Memphis in honour of this god was called Apide, or Apis, according to the Greek custom of forming the nominative case, which word in the enchorial language is seen to be the same as Pthah, PT or PD being the essential letters in each; Memphis, or rather Mem-phide, was the city of Aphide.

Seb, the father of the gods, and Thore the father of the gods distinguished by the *scarabæus*, are probably the same persons, and also probably the god whom Diodorus called Kronos, the father of Osiris, Isis, Typhon, Apollo, and Aphrodite. Here we find that the father of the gods is a much less important person than his son, a circumstance so peculiar that we must suppose that, in the case of Jupiter and Saturn, the Greeks borrowed it from Egypt. With respect to this god marrying his sister, it was an event so common in Egypt both with gods and kings, by the testimony of history and the hieroglyphics, that the words wife and sister appear to be confused. Three of the Ptolemies styled their queens sister when they were not so, probably meaning to imply that they were more than queens consort, and were fellow sovereigns with themselves.

Neith, the great mother of the Gods, is probably the goddess whom Diodorus called Rhea the mother of the gods. Plato (*Timæus*) says that Neith was worshipped at Sais, and called Minerva by the Greeks; but Plutarch (*De Iside et Osiride*) says that the Minerva of Sais was Isis: Cicero also (*De Nat. Deor.*) mentions the Minerva of Sais. Her name was the first syllable in the name of queen Nitocris, see Eratosthenes, page 82.

Osiris was worshipped all over Egypt; and, to judge by the number of votive tablets which are found dedicated to him, he must have been the chief object of worship, although only an inferior god or deified hero. He was the Dionysus or Bacchus of the Greeks; not the youthful god of wine, but the bearded Bacchus, the Egyptian conqueror of India beyond the Ganges, who first led an army into Asia, the son of Seb or Kronos, the husband of Isis, the father of Horus. Diodorus has preserved the following inscription to his honour: " Kronos the last of the gods is my father. I am Osiris the king, who led an army even to the uninhabited parts of India, and northward to the Danube, and on the other side to the ocean. I am the eldest son of Kronos, and the seed of beautiful and noble blood, and related to the day. I am everywhere, and help every body." He was the god of Amenti, the regions of the dead, and hence called, in an inscription quoted by

M. Letrone, Petemp-amentes, and in that character presided at the trial of the deceased, as seen on the papyri from the mummy cases, described at page 32.

Isis, his queen and sister, generally accompanies him. Herodotus and Diodorus considered her the same as Ceres, or the earth: her inscription quoted by Diodorus is as follows: " I am Isis the queen of the whole earth; I was taught by Hermes: what I bind no one can unloose. I am Isis the eldest daughter of Kronos the last god: I am the wife and sister of king Osiris: I first taught men to use fruits: I am the mother of Horus the king: I am in the constellation of the dog. The city of Bubastus was built by me: hail Egypt that nourished me." She sometimes has cows' horns, but more often a throne on her head. The Greek name and character of Io were borrowed from her, for Ioh (Ιοϩ,) is the Coptic for the moon, to which the cows' horns are an evident allusion. Lucian, however, who had lived in Egypt, ridicules this opinion, and makes Jupiter say ironically to Mercury, " carry Io into Egypt and make Isis of her." It was probably for the worship of this goddess that the Jews were reproved by Jeremiah (chap. xliv.) for burning incense to the Queen of Heaven. She is called Inachis by Ovid, in the following lines (*Metam.* ix. 686), where several of the gods are described:

" *Inachis* ante torum, pompâ comitata suorum,
   Aut stetit aut visa est; inerant lunaria fronti
   Cornua, cum spicis nitido flaventibus auro,
   Et regale decus: cum quâ latrator *Anubis*,
   Sanctaque *Bubastis*, variusque coloribus *Apis*;
   Quique premit vocem digitoque silentia suadet, [*Horus*]
   Sistraque erant, nunquamque satis quæsitus *Osiris*,
   Plenaque somniferi *serpens* peregrina veneni."

Indeed her names were latterly very numerous, and Fleetwood (*Inscriptionum Sylloge*) quotes an inscription

ISIDI. MYRIONYMÆ
FESTINUS

Horus, the son of Isis and Osiris, reigned on earth after his father; he was considered by Herodotus as the Apollo of the Greeks: he was also the Har-pocrates of the Greek mythology, both in name and character; he frequently has his finger on his mouth to represent that he is the god of silence. He is sometimes a child, forming with his father and mother a holy family, and when represented as a sitting figure with his hand to his mouth he is the hieroglyphic for *a child*; sometimes he has a large lappet from his head-dress hanging over his ear; sometimes he is a crowned eagle. His name Hor is Ουρο, the Coptic for *king*.

Aroeris is probably another name for this god; Plutarch says that some called him Apollo, and some the elder Horus: there is an inscription at Ombos Αροηρει θεῳ μεγαλῳ Απολλωνι. I should conjecture that the word Aroēris was Ουρο Ουρο, *Horus the king*, as he was emphatically called; as was Apollo in Homer, Απολλωνι ἀνακτι (Il. A. 36.)

Anūbis has a greyhound's head, and appears to be connected with the embalming of the mummies. Ovid calls him *latrator Anubis*. He was sometimes identified with Hermes, and is named in a Greek inscription quoted by M. Letrone, Ermes Pytnybis.

Athur was the Aphrodite or Venus of the Greeks: she was more particularly worshipped at Atar-bechis, which city was named after her. One of the months also was named after her. Her hieroglyphical name is No. 40, Plate V.

Thoth, the Lord of Letters, or of the Scribes, was the thrice-great

Hermes, Hermes Trismegistus, of the Greeks, the inventor of letters. The Ibis was sacred to him, and the first month in the year was named after him. No. 58, Plate V. is his name.

Nephthis is mentioned by Plutarch, but without any description. She is probably the goddess called Bubastis and Diana by Herodotus, though Diodorus considered Isis as Bubastis. On the votive tablets she is frequently the companion of Isis.

Pthah Sokar Osiris is a god frequently met with in the inscriptions; he is represented as a dwarf, and is no doubt meant by Herodotus (lib: iii. 37), when he mentions a pigmy statue of Vulcan.

The Nile was represented as a man with the breasts of a woman, sometimes with a beard; with a lotus on his head, a vase in his hand from which water flows. Herodotus remarks that the Egyptians did not worship Neptune; no doubt the Nile supplied his place.

Canōpus is mentioned by many authors, but is probably too modern a divinity to be met with in the inscriptions. Tacitus says that he was pilot to Menelaus; he was probably deified in the time of the Ptolemies. The priests of Canopus are said to have placed his head upon a water vase, that he might miraculously extinguish fire.

Serapis is another god of modern introduction, he was worshipped more particularly at Alexandria. His origin and attributes are imperfectly known; he was thought by Gibbon to have been brought from Sinope by Ptolemy Lagus: he soon became identified with Osiris, and was represented like a Jupiter with a basket on his head.

A group of four divinities, with the heads of a man, a mastiff, a greyhound, and a hawk respectively, is well known on the monuments; they appear to be connected with the future state; these heads are sometimes the covers to water pitchers, like the god Canopus, and are confounded with him.

Antæus is the Greek name for an Egyptian god, who gave his name to the city which the Greeks called Antæopolis; his Coptic name is unknown.

Typhon, a successor of Horus on the throne, is frequently mentioned by the Greek authors as an evil genius, but is not recognized on the monuments.

In addition to these, the sculptures present us with a variety of other divinities, such as a second god with the head of a greyhound, the companion of Anubis, three with the heads of hawks, a second with the head of the Ibis; none of which are easily distinguished. The Egyptians also, like the Hindoos, from whom they seem to have derived the idea, worshipped several triads or groups of three gods, as Isis, Osiris, and Horus; Nephthis, Isis, and Horus; and it was probably from Egypt that Plato derived that favourite number for the deity; see also Philo Judæus, who wrote at Alexandria.

Among the animals represented in the sculptures, as sacred objects, are the Cow, Ram, Greyhound, Hawk, Vulture, Ibis, a Fish, the Crocodile, Frog, Asp or thick-bodied snake, Crayfish, Scarabæus, and some few nondescript animals, such as the Sphinx.

One of the most frequent emblems on the sacred sculptures is the *crux ansata*, called by Plutarch Τυφωνος αιδοια, the character for *life*, which is most frequently held in the hand, as in Plate VI., sometimes is presented by a god to the mouth of a king, sometimes is brought down by a dove as a token of consecration.

Wings also are occasionally employed as emblems of divinity; thus we have winged goddesses, winged crowns, winged asps, winged suns.

In Bartoli's *Admiranda Rom. Antiq.* is a drawing of a Greco-Egyptian bas-relief, representing an Egyptian sacred procession, which, in almost all its particulars, agrees with the description of a procession in Clemens Alexandrinus (lib. vi.); the words of Clemens are as follows: " the singer walks first in the ceremony, carrying a symbol of music [the *sistrum*, fig. 70 of Plate V.]; they say that he ought to carry two of the books of Hermes, one containing the hymns of the god, the other the rules of life; after the singer walks the Horoscopus, who has in his hands a *horologium* and palm branch, symbols of astrology; he ought to have the four books of Hermes which treat of astrology always in his mouth: then follows the sacred scribe, having feathers on his head, books in his hands, and a ruler on which is ink, and a reed with which he writes; he ought to understand the hieroglyphics."

After this account of their mythology, we are led to wonder, in the words of Cicero, how priest could meet priest without laughing *quòd non rideat haruspex cùm haruspicem viderit*; but of the more important part of their religious and philosophical opinions, the little that we know is of a more enlightened kind; they believed in the immortality of the soul, as we learn from Herodotus, and in the rewards and punishments of a future state, as we may conclude from the various pictures of Osiris and the assessors presiding while the actions of the deceased are weighed in a scale. The solidity of their tombs, and the care employed in embalming the mummies, abundantly prove that they believed in the resurrection of the body; and though their belief in a ruling providence was disfigured and corrupted by the polytheism just described, yet that they held that important opinion we learn from their numerous tablets and sculptures.

On the Coptic Language.

THOUGH the Coptic alphabet, as we now have it, can only be traced back to about the first century of our era, the language itself appears to have existed from a very early period; it has no connexion with either the European or Hebrew families, but seems to have been distinctive of the sons of Mizraim of the book of Genesis, the inhabitants of the west side of the Red Sea. But Greek colonists appear to have settled in Lower Egypt at a very early time; and, after the conquest of the country by Alexander, and during the splendid dynasty of the Ptolemies, the Greek language must have taken deep root in the Delta. Consequently, when the early Christians translated the Bible into Coptic, they did it wholly through the medium of Greek, and it is from the Coptic versions of the Bible that we are best able to judge of the language. They were translated from the Greek version of the Septuagint and written from left to right, in Greek letters, except in those cases where the Coptic sound could not be expressed by any Greek letter of similar force. In the same way numerous Greek words are introduced where the translators could not find a Coptic word to express the meaning; and on all occasions the Greek words are used for Lord and God, as probably the Coptic words would have sounded rather idolatrously. The grammatical inflections are but few, the pronouns and articles are in the form of prefixes.

The Sahidic dialect, or that of Upper Egypt, had a few words peculiar to itself, but in all important particulars the Memphitic Coptic and the Sahidic Coptic were the same.

The alphabet, as printed, is as follows:

THE ALPHABET.

LETTERS DERIVED FROM THE GREEK.			LETTERS ONLY USED IN GREEK WORDS.		
Ⲁ	ⲁ	a	Ⲅ	ⲅ	g
Ⲃ	ⲃ	b	Ⲇ	ⲇ	d
Ⲉ	ⲉ	e short	Ⲍ	ⲍ	z
Ⲏ	ⲏ	e long	Ⲝ	ⲝ	x
Ⲑ	ⲑ	th	Ⲯ	ⲯ	ps
Ⲓ	ⲓ	i			
Ⲕ	ⲕ	k			
Ⲗ	ⲗ	l			
Ⲙ	ⲙ	m			
Ⲛ	ⲛ	n	LETTERS NOT IN THE GREEK ALPHABET.		
Ⲟ	ⲟ	o short	Ϣ	ϣ	ch, sh, s
Ⲡ	ⲡ	p	Ϥ	ϥ	f ?
Ⲣ	ⲣ	r	Ϧ	ϧ	k, g ?
Ⲥ	ⲥ	s and z	Ϩ	ϩ	h { the Greek aspirate.
Ⲧ	ⲧ	t and d	Ϫ	ϫ	y { z or j the first letter of Zoan or Tanis.
Ⲩ	ⲩ	u			
Ⲫ	ⲫ	ph	Ϭ	ϭ	s
Ⲭ	ⲭ	ch	Ϯ	ϯ	ti
Ⲱ	ⲱ	o long			

A few Coptic words may be here quoted as examples, and as showing the derivations of names met with in the foregoing pages, or which are familiar to us through the Old Testament or the Greek mythology.

THE COPTIC LANGUAGE.   135

Πλ, πεθ, π, ϕ, the definite article; hence Amenophis is called Phamenoph by Pausanias, so also perhaps the syllable *phe* in Potiphe-rah, *the priest of the Sun*, in Genesis.

Πι, πιθ, the plural article; hence possibly the names of several cities, as we say the Hague, the Porte; thus, Pi-beseth, Pith-om, Pi-hahiroth.

Ογρο, *king*; whence Horus the name of the god and of a king of Thebes; and with the article prefixed we have πλογρο, the well-known title Pharaoh, *The King*. Josephus tells us that Pharaoh simply meant *the king*.

Ρη, *the sun*, the name of the god Amun Ra; hence also Ra-meses Potiphe-rah: and probably the word *pyramid* may be πι ρη ϩιτωοτι, *the sun's paths*, or something similar; the pyramids being erected with strict regard to the sun's shadow at noon: and hence possibly the mistake of Pliny, who says (lib. xxxvi. 14) that the word *obelisk* signified in Egyptian, *the sun's rays*; he may have made the remark respecting the word *obelisk* which was true of the word *pyramid*.

Ιοϩ, *the moon*; hence the Greek goddess of that name.

Ⲙⲉⲉⲟⲛⲓ, *to take care of, to surround*; hence Jupiter Ammon and Amun Ra; hence also, taking the Septuagint as our guide, Memphis was called Amun No, the Great No, to distinguish it from No, Diospolis Parva (Nahum, iii. 8, נא אמון; Jerem. xlvi. 25, אמון מנא; Ezekiel, xxx. 15, המון נא). Amun was also used as a substantive for the name of the god instead of Amun Ra.

Ⲩⲉⲓ, *to love*, forms part of several kings' names and titles, particularly Amun-mai, *beloved by Amun*, the title of the Theban kings; as Memptah or Mei-m-Pthah, *beloved by Pthah*, was the title of the Memphitic kings.

Ⲩⲁⲧ, *mother*; Plutarch says μουθ.

Ⲉⲙⲙⲉⲛⲧ, *the habitation of the dead*; Plutarch says ἀμενθην: hence Petempamentis, a name of Osiris in a Greek inscription quoted by M. Letrone, *God of the regions of the dead.*

Ⲡⲓⲣⲱⲙⲓ, *a man*, repeated very remarkably by Herodotus without being understood by him; see page 18.

Ϣⲏⲣⲓ, *a son*, ϣⲉⲣⲓ, *a daughter*; hence the last syllables of many Egyptian names, as some of our own proper names end in -*son*, and the Roman family names all end in -*ius* or υἰος; thus in the preceding pages we have Chœres, Acen-cheres, Men-cheres, Bi-cheres, and others.

Ⲃⲁⲕⲓ or ⲟⲩⲃⲁⲕⲓ, *a city*, ⲑⲃⲁⲕⲓ or ⲑⲟⲩⲃⲁⲕⲓ, *the city*; having however a syllable more than Thebes, which I consider as derived from it: hence Atar-bechis, *the City of Athur.*

Ⲧⲁⲣⲃⲁ, Tapē, is the Coptic for Thebes, which the Greeks and Romans called Thebæ; the Arabic name is Medinet Abou, or perhaps more correctly Medineh Tabou, the city Tabou, Medineh being the Arabic for *city*. Champollion considered the word Tapē derived from the Coptic for *head* or *chief,* but the same syllables in the names of several cities are frequent enough to prove that Apē or Abou meant *city*; then Ⲧ being the Coptic article, Thebæ or Tapē would be *The City*. Papa, the name of another city, would mean the same, ⲡ being also the article; so Taposiris is literally *The City of Osiris*; the Arabs dropping the article called it Abousir, and the Greeks Busiris. The three cities Abydus, Abaton (Luean, x. 323), and This, if they are all different cities, appear to have at least the same monosyllabic name, to the first two of which the word Abou is prefixed; Abou-kir, Aboo 'l Haggag, Abou-tide, Aboogirgeh, begin with the same syllables. Hibe, the city in the great Oasis, is no doubt the same word; Aboo Simbel, a city in Ethiopia, begins with the same word.

Kaϩi, *the earth*; hence Eratosthenes (page 82) rightly explains the name Cho-mae-phthah, *the world beloved by Pthah*.

Uа is *a place*; ɴ is *of*; Ma-m-aphide is usually conjectured to be the derivation of Memphide, the *place of Apide* or *of Pthah*.

Ḣi, *a house*; hence Μεμνονειον, Memnon-eium, erroneously spelt Memnonium, *the palace of Memnon* or *of the beloved by Amun*. And analogy here suggests a derivation for Memphide quite as probable as the more usual one,—Mempthahei, or Mei-m-pthah-ei, *the palace of the beloved by Pthah*.

Χнɴɴ, *Egypt*, which is the same word as Ham, the son of Noah, who is called Χɑɴɴ in Coptic and Χαμ in the Septuagint. The word is also preserved in the name of the city Chemmis or Panopolis.

Ϣεɴɴɴω, *a stranger* or *captive*, which is the same word as Shem, the son of Noah: these two words strikingly agree with the account in the book of Genesis that the Egyptians were descended from Ham, and the Israelites, the strangers in their land, from Shem. Manetho adds that the Shepherd kings were called captives.

Uω, *water*; from which word Josephus says the name Moses was derived, meaning, *saved from the water*.

The use of the Greek preposition μετα in composition is peculiar and unclassical, thus

Κακος, *wicked*;   ⲙⲉⲧⲁⲕⲁⲕⲓⲁ, *integrity*. Ps. vii. 8.
Σεβας, *pious*;   ⲙⲉⲧⲁⲥⲉβⲏⲥ, *transgressions*. Ps. v. 10.
Πλεος, *full*;   ⲙⲉⲧⲁⲫⲗⲏⲟⲩ, *vanities*. Ps. xii. 2.

This would lead us to suspect that the unclassical word *metaphysics* was of Alexandrian origin; thus

Φυσικα, *material objects*; μεταφυσικα, *metaphysics*.

On the Ethiopic Language.

THIS language, as it exists in the translation of the Bible, has an alphabet of twenty-six letters, but as each letter is written in seven different ways, according to the vowel sound by which it is followed, and as these forms are in some cases very different from one another, it almost amounts to an alphabet of a hundred and eighty-two letters. It is written from left to right, but in other respects is closely connected with Hebrew and Arabic; its terminations and prefixes, and three quarters of its words, are considered as of that family. It does not contain the word *Pharaoh*, nor the article *pa, peth*, which are the Coptic peculiarities met with in the Pentateuch, and cannot be expected to be of use in hieroglyphical studies, but it becomes an object of great interest to enquire at what time this language migrated into Ethiopia. The more early Ethiopian language must have been the same as the Egyptian: Diodorus Siculus and Lucian (a very good authority), who both visited Egypt, agree in asserting the connection between the language, literature, and religion of the two countries; and the existing monuments prove that the Theban kings ruled over Ethiopia as their own country, at least down to the time of Rameses II. They ornamented it with buildings, statues, and sculptures, in the same style as they did Thebes, their own capital; the temples were dedicated to the same gods, and ornamented with similar inscriptions in hieroglyphics. Hence, until the time of Rameses II., Ethiopia was probably peopled by Copts. Possibly it was during the reigns of his less warlike successors that these Cushites succeeded in crossing the Red Sea; or perhaps some

THE ETHIOPIC LANGUAGE. 139

of the wars of Rameses II., carried on so successfully in Ethiopia, may have been, not against the Ethiopians, for they had been under the rule of his ancestors for three centuries, but against the encroachment of these Cushites, who two centuries later were masters of all Egypt. There are however two opinions respecting the race of men who inhabited Ethiopia when it was under the rule of the Theban kings. While the ancient writers inform us that the country was peopled by Copts, to whom the Egyptians were indebted for their civilization and literature, which is perhaps disproved by the inferiority of all the Ethiopian buildings, some modern writers have thought that the inhabitants of Ethiopia were Arabs or Cushites, ruled over as a conquered province by the Egyptian kings, which would seem equally disproved by our finding there the language, temples, and mythology of Egypt. The more probable opinion is that the Ethiopians were Copts, though inferior in the arts of civilization to the Egyptians; that the Cushites, crossing the southern end of the Red Sea, conquered Ethiopia after the time of Rameses II.; that these were the people who, under Sabbacon and his successors, conquered Egypt, and were known to the writers of the later books of the Old Testament as Cushites, and whose language we now possess in the Ethiopic version of the Bible. Perhaps the earliest certain information which we have of Ethiopia being peopled by Arabs is from Juba, who wrote his history of Africa about B. C. 30, and is quoted in page 96.

The passage in Ezekiel, xxix. 10, in which Egypt is defined in our common version as extending "from the tower of Syene to the border of Ethiopia [Cush]," is so important in a geographical point of view, that it ought not to be passed over. No ancient city is better known than Syene, in lat. 24° 8', exactly on the borders of Ethiopia, its latitude being the same as the sun's greatest northern declination.

"Umbras nusquam flectente Syene."—Lucan, ii. 587.

"Cancroque suam torrente Syenem."—Lucan, x. 234.

Hence some critics have supposed Arabian Cush was here meant, and have placed this at the northern end of the Red Sea. But in the Hebrew the passage is "from Migdol Syene, ממגדל סונה, to the borders of Cush," and in every case when the name of a place ends in ה like Syene, we are at liberty to suppose the preposition ה *to*, to be post-fixed, but omitted by what the grammarians call syncope, and thus the passage becomes "from Magdolus to Syene, on the borders of Ethiopia," a correct definition of the whole of Egypt.

There also is a remark on another part of our translation of the Old Testament, which belongs perhaps more properly to page 9, but may be introduced here; it is, that the confusion and division of languages mentioned in Genesis xi. seems to relate solely to the Sehemitic nations, or those who spoke dialects of Hebrew; the only alteration that I would propose in the translation is to leave the word Shem untranslated, and the passage will then stand thus:

V. 1. And all the world was of one language, [that is, all the district or land of Mesopotamia, as $\kappa o \sigma \mu o s$, Matt. iv. 8, and $\dot{\eta}$ οἰκουμενη, Luke, ii. 1, and iv. 5.] V. 4. And they said, let us build ourselves a city . . . . let us make us *Shem* [the name of the city]. V. 8. And the Lord scattered them abroad, [on the conquest of the city by the Assyrians under Nimrod, see Gen. x. 10 (page 8.)] V. 9. Therefore from that time was *Shem* called *Babel*, because the Lord did confound the language. . . . . . . V. 10. These are the generations of *Shem* [these are the tribes and dialects which took their rise at the dispersion of the nation which spoke Hebrew].

ON THE HIEROGLYPHICS AND HIERATIC WRITING.

THE knowledge of hieroglyphics which we at present possess owes its origin to the Rosetta Stone in the British Museum, which contains a decree in honour of King Ptolomy Epiphanes, in three characters. One of these is Greek, which, though defaced in parts and in some places obscure, has been pretty well explained by the sagacity of several critics; and in this portion it is stated that the decree was ordered to be written in Sacred, in Enchorial, and in Greek writing.

Dr. Young, by a careful comparison of the Greek with the hieroglyphics, counting the recurrence of the more marked characters with a degree of acuteness which those accustomed to decyphering will duly appreciate, determined first the name Ptolemy, and then allotted to each portion of hieroglyphical writing its portion of meaning, and, by a comparison of the recurrence of the same character in those different portions with the recurrence of the same Greek word, he was then able satisfactorily to allot to several other hieroglyphical characters their respective meanings. In many cases the meaning could only be affixed to larger groups of characters, and it is only by the discovery of the same characters occuring in other inscriptions, differently grouped with known characters, that the meaning has been affixt to individual characters. And in the same way, the meaning has been affixt to numerous other characters by a judicious selection of hieroglyphical sentences, in which a new character occurs in such connection with known characters, that only one meaning can be attributed to the new one.

This study has been pursued with considerable success by M.

Champollion, Mr. Wilkinson, and others, but there remains a large number of characters not yet understood, which is very little to be wondered at, when we consider that our knowledge of the language is derived from the translation of the decree upon the Rosetta Stone, which was written in Lower Egypt, B. C. 195, and that the other hieroglyphical inscriptions which we wish to read were written at various times during the preceding twelve centuries, and chiefly in Upper Egypt.

This language is written either from right to left or from left to right, and the columns are frequently so narrow that it may be almost said to be written from top to bottom. The reader in all cases reads in the direction that meets the faces of the animals represented in the sculpture. It is partly pictorial, thus, *an ox*, fig. 1; *a goose*, fig. 2; *a temple*, fig. 3, of plate V. are represented by the objects themselves; at other times, and even in the same sentence, it is phonetic, or spelt by an alphabet of about a hundred and forty letters. Many of these are of course synonymous, some being more suitable to hasty writing, others to ornamental sculpture; some being in use at an earlier, some at a later period. The force of these letters is determined by means of the names of the kings in which they are met with, but as this cannot be done very exactly they are most conveniently arranged under about twelve of our primary letters. Thus we cannot with certainty distinguish between the vowels, nor between P and Ph; G and K; D, T and Th; L and R; X is sometimes Ks, sometimes Sh. The alphabet has been so often published that it is unnecessary to repeat it, that in Mr. Wilkinson's *Materia Hieroglyphica* is the one which I should recommend.

The name of a king or queen is always in a ring or cartouche, as in plates III. and IV. The name of any other man or woman

HIEROGLYPHICS AND HIERATIC WRITING. 143

is distinguished by being followed by a sitting figure, thus fig. 4 is *a man*, fig. 5 *a woman*; in other cases there is no character to distinguish a letter from a symbol, an omission which we should be surprised at in any similar system of signals. Other words, however, were sometimes followed by a representation of the object meant, the meaning being expressed twice over, once by the word and once by the symbol; thus fig. 6 is the word *statue*, followed by the object itself; fig. 7 the word *priest*, followed by a tiger's head, the usual symbol of a priest; fig. 8 the word *wine*, followed by a bottle.

The phonetic and symbolical modes of writing are frequently united in the same word, as in the names Amun-mai and Ra-meses see H, plate IV.; Thoth-moses, 42, plate IV; so also in the word *ceremonies*, fig. 9, in which the most important part of the word is symbolic, while the grammatical termination of the noun is spelt: the same termination occurs in *sacred treasures*, fig. 10; *sacrifices*, fig. 11; and *blessings*, fig. 12. The peculiar serpent in fig. 11 is symbolical of immortality. Fig. 12 is very peculiar, the arrow being *good*, the mouth *of*, the next character *heaven*, and the rest being the termination of the noun. The plural termination in these groups is not always used; sometimes the character itself is repeated three times, as, in fig. 54, *the immortal gods*, where not only the hatchet for *god* is repeated, but also the asp, which is the adjective *immortal*: when a character only occurs twice the dual is meant, as in fig. 55, the *saviour gods*, meaning the deceased Ptolemy Soter and his queen. The words *kingdom*, fig. 13; *beloved*, fig. 14; *vase-bearer* fig. 15, have a different termination: *mother*, fig. 16; *statue*, fig. 17; *strength*, fig, 18, have another.

Some characters have been a good deal altered for the ease of the sculptor, thus, the female figure of Isis, fig. 21, is symbolical

of the word *heavens*, and as such, occurs spreading over the constellations in the Zodiac of Dendera; but it is more usually formed as fig. 22, as we have seen it in fig. 12; so, instead of the more elaborate form of a priest pouring out libations, fig. 19, we more frequently find fig. 20; and in the same way in fig. 15 and 46, a pair of legs is used instead of a man. In many other cases there was a more and a less ornamental form of the same word, thus fig. 23 and 24, each mean *son*, the egg being used for the goose; so in fig. 43 the eagle is crowned, in fig. 44 it is not.

But for the purpose of writing, there was a still less ornamental and more rapid way of forming the characters, which is always found in the MSS., and would naturally result from using a pen or style; this is called Hieratic Writing by Strabo and Pliny, the Hieroglyphics being, as the name implies, peculiar to sculpture. It would frequently be difficult to recognize in the hieratic characters, the resemblance to the object intended, without the hieroglyphics, which were the intermediate step; thus fig. 26 is the hieratic form of fig. 4; fig. 27 of the bird in fig. 10; fig. 28 of fig. 7; the whole having a poor and meagre appearance compared with the hieroglyphics.

Many of the phonetic words are found to be Coptic; thus fig. 29, 30, and 31 are each N, the Coptic prefix for the preposition *to*. Fig. 32 is P or Ph, and fig. 33 Peth, the prefix for the definite article; fig. 34 is the same, the B being used instead of P; fig. 35 is T, the same; fig. 36 is N K, ⲛⲭⲉ, the same; fig. 8 is ⲏⲣⲡ, *wine*; fig. 37 is M, the prefix for the preposition *of*; fig. 38 OTP, perhaps ⲱⲧⲉⲃ, *to go*. This group of characters occurs near the beginning of the votive tablets for the word *dedicated*, and is no doubt the last syllable of the name Amenothph, *devoted to Amun*. Fig, 39, ⲙⲟⲩ, *deceased*; fig. 14, ⲙⲉⲓ, *beloved*; fig. 16,

ⲙⲁⲩ, *mother*. But a still larger number of words, terminations, and prefixes, which are not found in Coptic, prove that this is at any rate a different dialect from what we now find in the versions of the Scriptures; and it may be as well to remark that, though many of the characters are thus illustrated and confirmed by a comparison with the Coptic words, none I believe have in the first instance been thus explained : in every case the agreement of the hieroglyphic with the Coptic word has only been seen after its meaning had been otherwise ascertained; indeed, very little reliance could be placed upon the translation of an hieroglyphic which rested on any other proof than a parallel translation, as on the Rosetta Stone, or on the rigid reasoning of the art of decyphering.

Some words, which it would be difficult to represent pictorially, are done so when taken syllable by syllable; thus, fig. 40 is an eagle, *the god Horus*, in a house with a window, which in Coptic is ⲏⲓ ⲧⲟⲩⲣⲟ, ei thouro, *the house of Horus*, and thus is made to represent the word Athori, the name of a goddess. In the enchorial language Horus is written Thorus, and in Eratosthenes (page 82), Taurus. Fig. 41 is a hand, frequently used to represent an enemy or captive; the hand was sometimes cut off and sent home as a trophy, though the value of a captive made this probably rather a figurative act than a real one. Fig. 42 is a hand, preceded by the word *cut off*, to express that upon this occasion it was done to the letter. Ⲭⲁⲭⲓ is the Coptic for *enemies*, ⲭⲓⲭ for *hands*; showing that the words were closely connected. Fig. 43 is ⲟⲩⲣⲟ, *king*, the eagle being the vowel and the ball R or Ra; this is a frequent title for *king*, and with the article ⲛⲁ prefixed is no doubt the word Pharaoh. The crown is that which is peculiar to Lower Egypt, and only an ornamental or symbolical addition. Fig. 44 is the same word with the addition of the female termination, and means *queen*.

Fig. 45 is a compound word, the two upper characters being *day*, the two lower *mother*, as in fig. 16, the whole being *mother-day*, or *birth-day*; fig. 46 is *day-bearing*, or *light-bearing*, being the well-known title of one of the Ptolemies, *Epiphanes* or *illustrious*. Fig. 47, 48, 49, 50 are the numerals—thousands, hundreds, tens, units. This mode of repeating each character as often as necessary is the same as what we call the Roman method of notation, while the Greeks and Hebrews used the letters of the alphabet, and had a different character for each of the units and tens: three thousand is used to represent many thousands. Fig. 51 is *Upper and Lower Egypt*, or literally the *Upper and Lower region*; the lower characters representing *the world*, and above are the crowns peculiar to Upper and Lower Egypt, which again occur on the figures in Plate III.; that at fig. 30 is of Lower Egypt, the other, of Upper Egypt, is mentioned by Diodorus as being worn by the priests in Ethiopia (see page 31). Fig. 52 is *priest-hood*; fig. 53 is *king-dom*: the last syllable in each of these words is very remarkable as a sign for an abstract idea; the sitting man, holding a crown upon his head, is also part of the words *gold, silver*, and *crown*. Fig. 54 is *the immortal gods*, the hatchet being *god*, the asp *immortal*; the asp distinguished the gods from the deified kings of fig. 55. Fig. 56 is a sceptre of common occurrence, also the letter Th; fig. 57 is *the moon*, 10ꜣ, or a vowel, perhaps A.

Enough has, I think, been seen to make it clear that, whatever may have been the origin of hieroglyphics, they have, as we now find them, no analogy with the Mexican picture-writing discovered by Humboldt. The Mexicans seem never to have known a method of expressing their words, they therefore attempted, by drawing, to express actions and ideas; the Egyptians, on the other hand, both could and did, when they pleased, express their words alphabetically: the Mexicans represented an idea, sentence, or action by a picture, but an Egyptian hieroglyphic represents a word or even a syllable, and these pictures run in sentences as words do: the difference is sufficiently clear between an action represented by a picture, and an action expressed in words, and those words represented by pictures.

Clemens Alexandrinus has left us (*Stromata*, v. 4) a description of the Egyptian mode of writing; the passage is as follows:

" Those who are taught by the Egyptians first learn that method of Egyptian writing which is called

> EPISTOLOGRAPHIC [enchorial], next the
> HIERATIC, which the sacred scribes use, and lastly the
> HIEROGLYPHIC; of this, one way is
> > *Phonetic* ($\kappa \nu \rho \iota o \lambda o \gamma \iota \kappa \eta$, express, not figurative) by means of the first letters, the other is
> > *Symbolic*; of the Symbolic, one is expressed
> > > *Imitatively*, another is written
> > > *Figuratively* ($\tau \rho o \pi \iota \kappa \omega s$), and a third way is
> > > *Like some riddles* ($\kappa \alpha \tau \alpha \ \tau \iota \nu \alpha s \ a \dot{\iota} \nu \nu \gamma \mu o \nu s$)."

This division of the subject is entirely explained by our present knowledge: the epistolographic or enchorial writing we shall hereafter consider, and shall then see that it is a distinct dialect of the language; the hieratic writing we have already mentioned as a variety of hieroglyphics, and, in this single particular, Clemens seems to be in error, in considering the hieratic entirely distinct, while the numerous manuscripts which we possess make it probable that it is merely a variety of hieroglyphics; the explanation and subdivision of the hieroglyphics seems peculiarly happy and complete.

The hieroglyphics which have been considered sufficiently explain the three modes of symbolic characters; 1st. the imitative is explained by fig. 1, 2, 3, &c. : 2d. the figurative, by fig. 21, Isis, for *the heavens*; fig. 46, light-bearing, for *illustrious*; fig. 51, the two crowns, for *upper and lower*; the sceptres to denote *power*: 3d. the enigmatical, which is like that kind of riddle which we call a *rebus*, is exemplified by fig. 40, *the house of Horus*, ei-thouro, Athuri; also by the words Ra-meses and Thoth-mosis of Plate IV.

The phonetic hieroglyphics, or the alphabet, is found quite to agree with the account of Clemens, that it was by means of first letters. The letters of the alphabet are found to be in many cases, and probably were in all, pictures of objects; and the force of the written letter was known from the Coptic word for the object, it being the first letter of that word. Thus the *globe* or *sun*, Ra (fig. 43), is the letter R; Ioh, *the moon* (fig. 57), is the letter I or A; Osiris (fig. 61), a vowel, O or A; the staff with the head of Anubis (fig. 68), a vowel, O or A; the globe quartered (fig. 51), ⲕⲁϩⲓ, *the earth*, or K. The musical instrument (fig. 70) called by the Greeks *sistrum*, and well known in the hands of the Greco-Egyptian statues, is the letter S.

The whole passage of Clemens is one of the most satisfactory that we possess, and in every respect agrees with our present knowledge of the subject. The epistolographic writing is what we shall hereafter consider under the name of enchorial, which is its more usual name, though it is sometimes called demotic.

In an exact and long document like the Rosetta Stone, it was found necessary to use the alphabet for a great many words, such as *when, where, who, with*, &c.; but in the case of many architectural and ornamental inscriptions, of which the subject was of the usual complimentary or dedicatory nature, the alphabet was very little made use of: indeed, when the inscription was used as an architectural frieze, the meaning seems to have been considered as second to the ornamental effect; the sentence was sometimes even begun in the middle, and written in each direction alike, for the sake of uniformity, the characters being reversed on the different sides of the centre.

On the Rosetta Stone we meet with the well-known Hebraism, " the gods *gave* him the *gift* of health," and " he *received* the *receipt* of the kingdom ;" a mode of expression which I have not met with in Coptic. The prepositions are used as in English, where they would be supplied in Latin or Greek by the inflections; thus, " carved in letters for priests," in five words, instead of *incisum literis hieraticis*; " statue of king," in three words, instead of *imago regis*.

I believe that all writers on hieroglyphics have considered the hook-formed character of fig. 16 as S; but we have seen that, in that group, it is more probably OU, the group being the word ⲟⲩⲁⲧ. The proof usually quoted is that it is the last letter of the name Ptolemæus; but a slight knowledge of Egyptian inscriptions will prove that the last letter of a Greek name must not be quoted to prove the force of the letter; and, in addition, a considerable number of Greek names are written in hieroglyphics in the genitive case, as Cæsaris Autocratoris, Berenices, Alexandros, Neocæsaris; the later names are more usually in the nominative, as Domitianus, Adrianus, Sebastus, &c. There is an inscription at Philæ in which the two modes are united, thus; Marcus Aureius (*sic*) Commodus Antoninou Autocratoris Cæsaris.

On the coins we find the Ptolemies always named in the genitive case, as, ΠΤΟΛΕΜΑΙΟΥ ΒΑΣΙΛΕΩΣ, ΘΕΩΝ ΑΔΕΛΦΩΝ; from which it seems not remarkable that in the hieroglyphical inscriptions the king should be named Ptolemæou.

In the case of other characters, there is a confusion between

150   HIEROGLYPHICS AND HIERATIC WRITING.

S and the vowels; thus the goose and the egg are each, I consider, sometimes an S, sometimes a vowel; they are usually considered S, but the egg (fig. 44) seems to be O ; and the goose is synonymous with the eagle in the title for *king* (see Plates III. and IV.). The same confusion between S and the vowels is found in the enchorial language, which makes it probable that the S was sometimes pronounced so indistinctly as to be overlooked.

HORUS APOLLO. The only work of antiquity that professes to explain hieroglyphical writing is one by Horus Apollo, who is believed to have been a grammarian of Alexandria, of the fourth century; and it is from this singularity, rather than from any merit that it possesses, that it claims our attention. It bears such internal evidence of being a tissue of nonsense, that it has generally been considered a spurious production of later ages. It is a small work in the Greek language; it contains, clause by clause, the explanation of single hieroglyphics, and frequently accompanied with the reason for the character having such a meaning, always founded upon figurative considerations. The greater part of these characters never occur in the hieroglyphical inscriptions which have come down to us, and, as the meanings attributed to them are such that it is incredible that they could have existed on the monuments at all, the work has always been rejected as worthless. But now that by modern ingenuity, guided by the sure and philosophical rules of induction, we have some slight knowledge of hieroglyphics, we are led by a natural curiosity to compare such knowledge with the assertions of Horus Apollo; not expecting to gain any information from him,—for it would be unphilosophical to rely upon a witness whose testimony, whether from ignorance or willfulness, is false in ninety-nine cases out of an hundred,—but to see whether he had any knowledge at all of the subject which he professed to teach. The conclusion we arrive at is, that, though the author has produced a most clumsy fabrication, yet, from a few of his explanations being correct, he must have associated with or been instructed by the Egyptian priests, or some one who understood the subject. He mentions

Eternity, as represented by a Serpent whose tail is rolled up and covered by the rest of his body, and this they make of gold, and place round the image of their gods: this I consider the asp of the Rosetta Stone (Plate V. fig. 54,) where it distinguishes the immortal gods who govern the world from the saviour gods (fig. 55,) who are the deceased Ptolemies.

To a Vulture, amongst other meanings, he gives the word mother: in which sense it frequently occurs, for instance in the title Philometer.

A Goose means son: see fig. 23 and 24.

A month is sometimes denoted by the Moon turned downwards: which occurs repeatedly on the Rosetta Stone as part of the groups for *monthly*, and for the names of the months (see fig. 57, see also Plate VI.)

Very probably there may be several other correct explanations given, but these are enough to establish that the author had acquired some information from the Egyptian scribes; and it is quite unnecessary to produce instances to show that the great portion of his work is a tissue of nonsense.

On the Enchorial Language.

THE Rosetta Stone contains, beside the hieroglyphic and Greek inscriptions, a third, in a language which is called in the Greek the *enchorial* writing, γραμματα εγχωρια. It is, I believe, chiefly to Dr. Young that we owe the little knowledge which we have of this language. The ingenuity which could decypher the hieroglyphics could of course translate the enchorial writing, and the knowledge thence gained was further increased by the discovery of two or three papyri in the same characters, accompanied with a Greek translation. This language is frequently found on the papyri of the mummy cases; it seems to be more modern than the hieratic, but its origin is uncertain, and there is not evidence enough to prove, what has been with probability conjectured, that it is merely hieratic writing gradually altered by lapse of time, and by the necessity of adopting a more rapid mode of forming the hieroglyphical character. But while the hieroglyphic and the hieratic character in some cases approach so near to one another that they only differ in as much as the one is carefully carved with an attention to beauty, and the other rapidly written with a style or pen, the same cannot be said of the enchorial character, for though some few hieroglyphics are observed in the middle of the alphabetical writing, the manuscripts at present discovered do not show a passage from one mode of writing to the other. This language is written from right to left, and generally in a running hand, the characters being united in a manner which adds to the difficulty of decyphering an unknown language.

The earliest dates discovered on these papyri are of Psammetichus, about B. C. 650; some also bear the date of Darius, but the greater number bear the name of the Ptolemies, and it is from these latter ones that the knowledge of the language is derived; hence we cannot be surprised that this, which was the vulgar tongue of Lower Egypt, after the Ethiopian invasion—after the country had been for two hundred years a province of Persia, and while under a race of Greek kings, should differ a good deal from the Coptic of Upper Egypt.

From the Greek proper names an alphabet has been formed; that in Plate VI. is nearly the same as Dr. Young's, though differing in a few instances, the letters are there arranged partly according to their resemblance to one another, and the following words in which they occur may be quoted to prove the force of each.

A. *Alexander, Antigenes, Arsinoë, &c.*
O long. 1. *Osoroëris, Petosiris;* 2. *Petophoïs;* 3. *Soter;* 4. *Soter, Cæsar.*
P, Ph. 1. *Ptolemy, Cleopatra;* 2. *Pechytes, Panas;* 3. *Psenamon, Peteutemis;* 4. *Phibis, Petosiris;* 5. *Psenchonsios;* 6. *Ptolemy, Cleopatra;* 7. *Ptolemy,* also for No. 6; *Soter,* for as this cannot be an *S,* we must suppose they pronounced the word rather differently; 8. *Ptolemy.*
K, Ch. 1. *Cleopatra, Nechmonthis;* ⲬⲎⲘⲒ (Egypt), *Autocrator;* 2. *Cleopatra, Antigenes;* 3. *Cæsar;* 4. *Antimachus, Cleopatra, Cæsar;* 5. *Cleopatra, Berenice;* 6. probable; 7. *Cæsar, Cleopatra, Autocrator.*
Sn, Sm. 1. *Zminis;* 2. *Snachomeneus;* 3. *Snachomes;* 4. *Pacemios.*
B. 1. *Berenice, Lubais;* 2. *Phabis, Berenice;* 3. *Phibis.*
G, K. 1 and 2. *Aleksandros, Berenice;* 3. *Antigenes, Alegsander, Cleopatra.*

D, T. 1. *Aetus, Cleopatra, Ptolemæus*; 2. *Antigenes, Alexandros*; 3. *Diogenes, Tolemæus*, for *Ptolemæus*; 4. *Alexandros*; 5. *Thynabunum*; 6 and 7, the definite article; at the beginning of a date.

H. Th. 1. *Horus*; 2. *Horus, Nechmonthis*; 3. *Thebais*; 4. *Thebais*; 5. *Petosiris*, Tsh for Ch in *Chimnaraus*.

M. 1. *Amonius*; 2. *Muthes, Ptolemæus*; 3. Uei (beloved).

N. 1. *Antimachus, Alexander, Berenice*; 2. *Arsinoë, Psenamon*; 3. *Psenamon*; 4. probable; 5. *Alexander*; 6. probable.

Ch. 1. Chapocrates, Cleopatra; 2. Chapocrates.

R. 1. *Sempoëris, Osoroëris*; 2. *Horus*; 3. *Cleopatra, Horus*.

L. *Alexander, Ptolemæus*.

Sh. 1. probable; 2. probable; 3. *T*sh for Ch in *Chimnàraus*; 4. *Osoroëris, Phabis*; 5. for the last; 6. *Aetus,* συνταξειΣ.

S. 1. *Aleksandros*; 2. *Aleksandros*; 3. *Psenchonsis, Psenamunis*; 4. *Autocratoris, Cæsaris*, Plate VI.

S. 1. *Arsinoë, Cæsaros*; 2. for the former.

I. 1. *Arsinoë, Syntaxeis*; 2. *Arsinoë*; *Ptolemæus, Berenice, Cæsar*.

U. 1. *U* (and); *Ptolemæou, Arsinoë*; 2. *Ptolemæou, Neksho* (king).

O short. 1. *Ptolemæus, Cleopatra, Alexandros*; 2. *Autocrator*; 3. *Apide* (*Apis*).

Œ. 1. *Diogenes, Eirene*; 2 and 3, the last letter, in some papyri, of Cleopatra, Ptolemæose, Alexandrose, Berenice; 4. *Arsinoë*.

Ei. 1. *Eireos, Pheibios*; 2. *Eirios, Irene*; 3. ні (a house); 4. *Eirene*.

Of these letters some few may be traced in the hieratic writing; thus, Sn is perhaps the sitting figure fig. 26 of Plate V. M may be compared with fig. 37. By comparing the enchorial and hieroglyphic name of Horus it would appear that the second R is the whip which is held as a sceptre (see some of the figures in the Tablet of Abydus, Plate III.): other resemblances may be traced, but not sufficient to establish a connection between the two modes of writing.

Some few hieroglyphics do certainly occur, such as *for ever* and *year*, No. 10, Plate VI.; and the similarity between words so unlike as *God*, No. 19; *Ra*, No. 22; *Pthah*, part of No. 23; *Athur*, No. 24; *Osiris*, No. 25, proves that the tall character O is used symbolically of divinity. No. 20 is *gods*; No. 21 the *saviour gods*, Ptolemy Soter and his queen, in which the horizontal stroke across the O has the effect of introducing the hieroglyphical character for Soter of Plate V. fig. 55.

Proper names generally begin with a curved stroke which appears to be the letter N; thus, No. 1 is Nalksndrosoe, *Alexander*; No. 2, Nptlomisoe, *Ptolemy*; No. 3, Nkloptroe, *Cleopatra*; No. 4, Narsinoe, *Arsinoë*; No. 5, Nbrnikoe, *Berenice*; in all of which names the uniformity of the termination proves that it is difficult to determine the force of a final letter: No. 6 is Aotœkrtors, *Autocratoris*; No. 7, Kisris, *Cæsaris*; No. 8 is Sntksis, συντάξεις, *taxes*, which word it seems they did not venture to translate on the Rosetta Stone; No. 9, Pootroe, meant for the title *soter*.

In the same way a few other words may be spelt which are not proper names, and of these a sufficient number are Coptic to prove that the enchorial writing is based upon that language; thus No. 11 is eoe, ⲟⲟⲧ, day; and this contraction is proved by the two ways in which the name Pyrrhius is written, in which these are the last two vowels. No. 12 is *Athur*, spelt as we have seen the hieroglyphical character fig. 40 in Plate V. the O being symbolical of god, meant for Horus, and the EO or EI, ⲕⲓ, the *house*; the house of

Horus, Ei-thor or Athur. No. 13 is *Priests*; No. 14 is *Opdo, Apide*, or *Apis*; No. 15, Opdieo, or Apid-ei, *the house of Apis*; used however generally for a temple of any god, a circumstance which would show that the language belonged to Lower Egypt, where Apis or Pthah was the great god.

But on the other hand the letter U is the conjunction *and*, a word so important that from it alone we might venture to conjecture that the Ethiopian conquerors and Arabic Shepherd Kings had left some trace of their language in this mixed dialect, U being *and* in Ethiopian as well as Hebrew. No. 16 is Nkshu, *a king*; a word that is not Coptic, but may be found in the Ethiopic language, where Negshy has that meaning; No. 17 is Oksho-ei, *the house of the king*, or *a city*; from which we learn that the N is not a radical part of the word Nekshu, and which shows that it is not very unlike Hyksos, the name that Manetho gives to the Arabic Shepherd Kings.

Of No. 23, the first half is symbolic of *Pthah*, the latter half is mo, or ⲙⲉⲓ, *beloved*, the whole being Pthah-mei, *beloved of Pthah*, a title taken by most of the kings of Lower Egypt, who were crowned in the temple of Pthah. No. 18 is Chmu or ⲭⲏⲙⲉⲓ, *Egypt*. The sentence at the bottom of the plate may be given as a specimen; the words are divided by the strokes underneath; it is, *In the* year six *of the* god, *the* son *of a* god *and of a* goddess, *the* victorious Autocratoris *Cæsaris*, &c., which is the beginning of a sentence in the middle of a tablet of the time of Cleopatra, published in the hieroglyphics of the Egyptian Society, plate 74.

In conclusion, it appears that the language of Upper Egypt and Ethiopia, at the earliest period to which our inquiries reach, was Coptic, written in hieroglyphics; with respect to the language of

THE ENCHORIAL LANGUAGE. 157

Lower Egypt at that early time we have no evidence, as its inhabitants have left no sculptures, but as it had been ruled over by an Arab or Phenician race of shepherds, and had at all times been partially colonized by Greeks, we may suppose that its language was not unmixed.

About B. C. 700, Egypt was conquered by an Arab race which had previously conquered Ethiopia, and it is soon after this, on the transfer of the seat of government to Lower Egypt, that we first meet with the enchorial language of that region, but hardly in sufficient quantity to trace its peculiarities. Egypt was then made a province of Persia for two hundred years, and it was then that the manuscripts on papyrus were first formed, from which we gain our knowledge of the enchorial language, and we find that though Coptic in most respects, it has some Ethiopic peculiarities.

Under the Greek kings we find a Coptic alphabet invented, the letters of which are chiefly borrowed from the Greek, and some deficiencies in the language are supplied from the same source, but with this exception the Coptic language appears to be pure and unmixed. And lastly, we meet with the alphabet and language of the Ethiopians, or rather of the Arabic conquerors of Ethiopia, of which three quarters of the words are Arabic, though written from left to right; and this language, with its Arabic neighbour, must from this time have continued to gain ground in Egypt, as it was probably several centuries before the Arab conquest of Egypt, in A. D. 640, that it was found necessary to add an Arabic translation to each page of the Coptic Bible, a custom which has been followed to the present day.

On the Date of the Trojan War.

MITFORD, in his History of Greece, considers the time of the Trojan War to be best determined by the following circumstances.

1st. Before the Trojan War, the descendants of Pelops had succeeded in expelling the descendants of Hercules, and at that time the reigning families of nearly all Greece were of the Pelopidan race, indeed Homer only mentions three Heracleidan kings as joining in the expedition against Troy. Thucidides tells us that it was about eighty years after the Trojan War that the Heracleidæ returned, and this is confirmed by Pausanias, lib. iv. 3; they made themselves sovereigns over all the Peloponnesus, except Arcadia and Achaia, expelling the Pelopidan dynasties in their turn. Now, since the whole of the Iliad and Odyssey relate entirely to the actions of the Pelopidæ, and there is no mention of an event so important as their expulsion, we must conclude that these poems were written within eighty years of the events described; and as Herodotus says, lib. ii. 53, that Homer lived 400 years before his own age, and Herodotus was born 484, B. C., and wrote about B. C. 430, we have the Trojan War dated in rather general terms about B. C. 900.

2dly. One of these returning Heracleidan kings was Oxylus, to whom Eleia was allotted. His *descendant* Iphitus (Pausanias, v. 4) established the Olympic games, and since, during the first centuries after Christ, the method of dating by the Olympiads and the Christian era were jointly used, the first Olympiad is well known to be B. C. 776.

Sir Isaac Newton and Mitford agree in *conjecturing* that Iphitus was only the grandson of Oxylus, and this is founded principally upon the absence of events to fill up the time of a greater number of generations; hence, if we add to 776 B. C. the 80 years which passed between the Trojan War and Oxylus the Heracleid's coming to the throne of Eleia, and about 50 years more for the interval till his grandson established the Olympic games, we again have about B. C. 900 for the date of the Trojan War.

In addition to these, I would mention the following arguments in favour of this interpretation of Herodotus and Manetho, and in opposition to Diodorus Siculus and Eratosthenes, who place the Trojan War more than two centuries earlier.

3dly. Manetho says that Thuoris, who reigned seven years, lived in the time of the Trojan War, and that he was succeeded by the 20th dynasty, that reigned together 135 or 172 years. Now we are led to conjecture, but it is a conjecture confirmed by many circumstances, that the 21st, 22d, 23d, and 24th dynasties that reigned in distinct places, did not succeed the 20th, but reigned contemporaneously with it. Granting this, Sabbacon succeeded, who reigned 8 years, and Sevechus who reigned 14; hence, from the middle of the reign of Thuoris to the middle of that of Sevechus is, taking the mean of the differing periods, 172 years, and, if we add this to 730 B. C., the time when So, or Sevechus, was king of Ethiopia in the 12th year of the reign of Ahaz, we again have about B. C. 900 for the time of the Trojan War. This by no means rests singly upon the conjecture that So is Sevechus, for it would equally well be established by granting that Tarachus is the same as Tirhakah, or Nechao II. the same as Pharaoh Nechoh; the conjecture that it rests upon is that the dynasties of Bubastus, Sais, and Tanis were contemporary with those of Thebes, as represented in the chart, Plate I.

DATE OF THE TROJAN WAR.

4th. Herodotus says that Proteus was contemporary with the Trojan War, and that between him and the Persian invasion of Egypt there were twelve reigns, of which he mentions the length of some, and, if we allow twenty-two years and a half for the length of those which he has left indefinite, we find (see page 26) the middle of the reign of Proteus falls B. C. 925.

5th. Herodotus says that there was only one reign between Sesostris the conqueror of Palestine and Proteus the contemporary of the Trojan War; hence, from the middle of the reign of Sesostris to the middle of that of Proteus was forty-five years, at twenty-two years and a half a reign. Now, if Sesostris be allowed to be the same as Shishak who conquered Jerusalem in the fifth year of the reign of Rehoboam, or B. C. 960, we have B. C. 915 for the time of the Trojan War.

This last determination is very valuable, as being obtained on the same series of reigns as the 4th, but in the reversed order, in one the known date being before, in the other after the Trojan War. One checks the other; if the length of reigns be taken too long or too short, the error would in one case put the war too early, in the other too late. It may be remarked that these determinations of an event measured along the reigns of the Egyptian kings, certainly in the case of Herodotus, who was well acquainted with the history of his own country, and probably also in the case of Manetho, are independent of the truth of Egyptian history. All that we have to remark is, that the historian, when counting the reigns of a certain race of kings, whether true or fabulous, back from his own time, or from some other known time, tells us that this one was contemporary with the Trojan War. We have only to determine of what length each reign was understood to be by the historian, for he spoke of the number of reigns as we

DATE OF THE TROJAN WAR. 161

do of the number of years; and also the date of one of the known reigns, or events mentioned.

6th. 1 Kings, xvi. 29: Ahab king of Israel marries [about B. C. 918] Jezebel, daughter of Ethbaal [or Ithobalus] king of the Zidonians. We find from the Tyrian annals, as handed down by Menander (see Josephus against Apion), that Ithobalus reigned 32 years and died aged 68, Badezorus reigned 6, Margenus reigned 9, and seven years after his death Dido fled and built Carthage. Now, if we suppose that Ahab came to the throne ten years before the death of his father-in-law Ithobalus, we have Carthage founded B. C. 886; and, if we rely on the tradition on which Virgil rested in the Æneid, we have that date for the destruction of Troy.

Again, 7th. Pausanias gives us several genealogies, out of which we may form a chain which will connect the Trojan War with a known date. Lib. ii. 18, Tisamenus, the son of Hermione the daughter of Menelaus, was king of Sparta at the time of the return of the Heracleidæ, when among others Temenus entered the Peloponnesus. Lib. ii. 13, Rhegnidas, the son of Phlax the son of this Temenus, is opposed by Hippasus in his invasion of Phlias. And Pythagoras the Wise was the son of Mnesarchus, the son of Euphron, the son of Hippasus. Thus, as Hermione was born at the time of the Trojan War, and Temenus was the contemporary of Tisamenus, and Hippasus of Rhegnidas, we have

Trojan War = Birth of Hermione
     Tisamenes = Temenus
          Phlax
     Hippasus = Rhegnidas
     Euphron
     Mnesarchus
     Pythagoras.

DATE OF THE TROJAN WAR.

Thus, at 39 years for a generation, we find the birth of Pythagoras was 234 years after the Trojan War. Now the time of Pythagoras is pretty well known; Pliny, lib. ii. 6, says that it was about the 32d Olympiad [B. C. 648] that he discovered that the planet Venus moved between the sun and the earth, and, as Sir Isaac Newton remarked, the circumstance that a transit of Venus across the sun did happen at that time is a coincidence so strong that we cannot but believe that Pythagoras observed it, and that it was from this observation that he learned that Venus passed between the earth and the sun; and that Pliny quoted an authentic record when he assigned the 32d Olympiad for the date.

By Vince's solar and planetary tables, I find that for the longitude of Egypt and Asia Minor, on the 16th of November, B. C. 643, or rather on the year which preceded the year A. D. 1800 by 2443 Gregorian years, the longitude of Venus's node was 233° 50', and that Venus and the sun were in conjunction in longitude 234° 42', five hours and a half before noon on that day, when, as the latitude of Venus was only 3', the planet must have passed very nearly across the centre of the sun, and the transit must have lasted nearly all day. Eight years later, B. C. 635, there was another transit, on the 13th of November, of which the middle was at eight o'clock in the evening, after sunset; at that time the longitude of the node was 233° 54', of the conjunction 232° 14', when the latitude of Venus was about 6', and the transit began about noon. As of course no other transit took place within 105 years, either before or after these, the coincidence with Pliny's date is striking, and I think conclusive. If Pythagoras was about forty years old at this time, he would have been born B. C. 680, which places the Trojan War at B. C. 910. Those who wish to see the arguments in favour of placing the Trojan War three centuries earlier may consult the notes to Larcher's Herodotus.

On the Date of the Jewish Exodus.

The accession of a king or dynasty in Lower Egypt, about the time of the birth of Moses, "who knew not Joseph," and had no recollection of his services, is an event so nearly agreeing in circumstances and in time with the expulsion of the Shepherd Kings, mentioned by Manetho, that it is worth while to examine the history in the Old Testament, to know how accurately the time can be determined. The commonly received theory is, that David died 475 years after the Exodus. On an examination of the passages, we shall find that this is in part conjectural: some events are not very closely connected with others; some periods are of uncertain length, which different readers will estimate differently; and other periods are of forty years, which is not meant as a definite number of years.

Exodus, vii. 7.—Moses was eighty years old when he spake unto Pharaoh.

Numbers, x. 11.—In the second year of the Exodus, the Israelites encamped in the wilderness of Paran, and it was from Kadesh in the same wilderness, and no doubt in the same year, (Numb. xiii.) that Joshua and Caleb were sent forward to espy the land.

Joshua, xiv. 7.—Caleb tells Joshua that this event was forty-five years ago; Caleb was eighty-five years old when he said this, and he survived Joshua, who however lived to be 110; let us suppose that Joshua lived ten years after that conversation.

Judges, iii. 8.—After the death of Joshua, the people did evil, and were subject to the king of Mesopotamia for eight years.

Judges, iii. 11.—They were then ruled over by Othniel the son of Kenaz the younger brother of Caleb, for forty years. This makes Othniel's death take place 143 years after the birth of his uncle Caleb.

Judges, iii. 14.—The Israelites did evil, and served the king of Moab for eighteen years. Ch. iii. 15; iv. 1.—Ehud delivered them and ruled over them till he died, say for twenty years.

Judges, iv. 3, 24.—They served Jabin, king of Canaan, for twenty years, till they put him to death.

Judges, v. 31.—On Deborah's delivering the land, it had rest for forty years.

Judges, vi. 1.—The Lord delivered them into the hand of Midian for seven years.

Judges, vi. 2; viii. 28.—Gideon ruled forty years, till he died of a good old age. Ch. ix. 22.—Abimelech reigned three years.

Judges, x. 2.—Tola judged twenty-three years. 3.—Jair judged twenty-two years. 8.—They served the Philistines eighteen years.

Judges, xii. 7.—Jephthah judged Israel six years. 9.—Ibzan judged seven years. 11.—Elon judged ten years. 14.—Abdon judged eight years. Ch. xiii. 1.—They were then delivered into the hands of the Philistines for forty years.

The whole of the history of Samson, who judged Israel twenty years *under the Philistines*, till the destruction of the temple of Dagon, I consider to be included in these forty years. I also consider the forty years during which Eli judged Israel (1 Sam. iv. 18), as either wholly or partly included in the forementioned period.

1 Sam. vii. 13, 15.—In Samuel's days the temple of Dagon was overthrown, and then the Philistines were beaten, and he judged Israel all his life, and made his sons judges when he was old (ch. viii. 1.) He judged nearly all through Saul's reign, and died about the time of David's marriage, (1 Sam. xxv.) [suppose forty years after the

DATE OF THE JEWISH EXODUS. 165

defeat of the Philistines, as he was young when the Philistines were beaten]. David soon after succeeded to the throne, and reigned forty years. If we put these together, we have

From the birth of Moses to the Exodus	80 years.
To the espying of the land	2
To Caleb's conversation	45
To Joshua's death (assumed)	10
Servitude	8
Othniel ruled	40
Servitude	18
Ehud judged (assumed)	20
Servitude	20
Deborah's rest	40
Servitude	7
Gideon	40
Abimelech	3
Tola	23
Jair (grandson of Hezron the grandson of Judah)	22
Servitude	18
Jephthah (grandson of Machir the grandson of Joseph)	6
Ibzan	7
Elon	10
Abdon	8
Servitude under the Philistines	40
To Samuel's death and David's marriage (assumed)	40
To Saul's death (assumed)	3
To David's death	40
Total, from the birth of Moses	550 years.

DATE OF THE JEWISH EXODUS.

It is sufficient for the purpose of comparison with Manetho's chronology to remark that there is here considerable uncertainty. This space of time might be made longer by supposing an interval between Samuel and the servitude under the Philistines: on the other hand it would be much more easy to shorten the period, by remarking that five of these periods are stated in round numbers to be forty years each, and one to be eighty years; and that some of the events which are here made to succeed one another may possibly have happened at the same time.

To compare with this history we have several genealogies, and to make use of these, I remark that one hundred names, taken as they come out of the English Peerage, give us the age of the father, - at the birth of his eldest child, 32 years,
———————————————— youngest, 46 years.
Taking the mean of these, we have 39 years for the length of a generation, from birth to birth, and in proof of this we may quote the generations in Genesis xi.; from the birth of Arphaxadad, two years after the flood, to the birth of Abraham, there are eight generations, or 290 years, being thirty-six and a quarter each upon an average. In this way we have the time between the birth of Jacob and the birth of the following:

Moses,	1 Chron. vi. 3	4 gen.,	156 years.
Jair,	1 Chron. ii. 22	6	234
Jephthah,	Judges xi. 1; 1 Chr. vii. 14	5	195
David,	1 Chron. ii. 15	11	429
Asaiah,	1 Chron. vi. 30	9	351
Ethan,	1 Chron. vi. 44	14	546
Zadok,	1 Chron. vi. 8; xv. 11	14	546
Asaph,	1 Chron. vi. 39	14	546

The last four were singers in David's Temple.

Now the whole of these genealogies tend to show that we have made the number of years in page 165, between the birth of Moses and death of David, too great by nearly 200, and to make it probable that we have there set down intervals of time as following one another, which in reality were included one in the other. Hence I prefer relying solely upon the royal genealogy of David, important as it afterwards became, and which is quoted in Ruth, Chronicles, Matthew, and Luke. This, at 39 years for a generation, and with B. C. 1015 for the death of David, gives us the following *approximate* dates:

$$
\begin{aligned}
\text{The birth of Abraham} &\quad 1592 \text{ B. C.} \\
\text{Joseph} &\quad - \quad 1475 \\
\text{Moses} &\quad - \quad 1358 \\
\text{David} &\quad - \quad 1085
\end{aligned}
$$

A Chronological Table of Events connected with Egyptian History.

B. C.
- 970. In the fifth year of Rehoboam, Shishak takes Jerusalem.
- 776. The beginning of the Olympiads.
- 729. In the twelfth year of Ahaz, Seve is king of Egypt.
- 707. In the nineteenth of Hezekiah, Tirhakah is king; and Sennacherib invades Egypt.
- 608. Pharaoh Nechoh kills Josiah king of Judah.
- 588. Zedekiah, in the ninth year of his reign, treats with Pharaoh Hophra.
- 525. Cambyses conquers Egypt.
- 522. Smerdis reigns seven months.

521.	Darius Hystaspes.
485.	Xerxes I.
464.	Artaxerxes Longimanus comes to the throne.
424.	Xerxes II. reigns two months.
424.	Sogdianus reigns seven months.
423.	Darius Nothus or Ochus.
410.	Amyrtæus makes himself independent.
362.	Nectanebus invades Judæa; Tachus comes to the throne.
358.	Darius Ochus comes to the Persian throne.
351.	Darius Ochus conquers Nectanebus II.
337.	Arses, his son, comes to the throne.
335.	Darius Codomanus.
330.	Alexander conquers Memphis.
323.	Ptolemy Soter.
283.	Ptolemy Philadelphus, alone.
247.	Ptolemy Euergetes.
222.	Ptolemy Philopater.
205.	Ptolemy Epiphanes, alone.
181.	Ptolemy Philometor.
146.	Ptolemy Euergetes II., alone.
117.	Lathurus and Cleopatra.
81.	Ptolemy Auletes.
51.	Cleopatra.

THE END.

MAGISQUE NATURÆ INDUSTRIAM HOMINUM QUAM VIM AUT TEMPUS DEESSE.

SALLUST.

www.ingramcontent.com/pod-product-compliance
Lightning Source LLC
Chambersburg PA
CBHW060837170426
43192CB00019BA/2803